MANAGEMENT

Level 3

by

JILL BLACKLIN MBA DMS CertEd

Published by:
The Institute of the Motor Industry
Fanshaws
Brickendon
Hertford
SG13 8PQ

© 1997 The Institute of the Motor Industry

ISBN 1 871880 34 3

Publications Manager: Peter Creasey FIMI
Education Manager: Alan Mackrill MBA BEd(Hons) LAE FIMI AssIPD
Series Editor: Harry Darton BSc(Econ)

Designed by: Julian Bennett, Hertford

Originating, printing and binding in Great Britain by:
Black Bear Press Ltd
Kings Hedges Road
Cambridge
CB4 2PQ

THE UNDERPINNING KNOWLEDGE SERIES

Books in the Underpinning Knowledge series, published by The Institute of the Motor Industry, are:

MANAGEMENT Level 3
by Jill Blacklin CertEd,DMS,MBA   ISBN 1 871880 34 3

VEHICLE BODY REPAIR
by Allan Rennie LAE MIMI   ISBN 1 871880 24 6

CUSTOMER SERVICE in the Motor Trade
by Bill Naylor FIMI   ISBN 1 871880 39 4

VEHICLE PARTS Administration and Organization
by Tom Colley LAE MIMI   ISBN 1 871880 14 9

VEHICLE MECHANICAL AND ELECTRONIC SYSTEMS
by Andrew Livesey BEd(Hons),IEng,LAE,FIMI   ISBN 1 871880 19 X

VEHICLE FINISHING
by Charles Long MIMI   ISBN 1 871880 29 7

Enquiries regarding this series and orders for the books should be addressed to:

Publications Manager
The Institute of the Motor Industry
Fanshaws
Brickendon
Hertford
SG13 8PQ
Tel: 01992 511521
Fax: 01992 511548

AUTHOR'S NOTES

The purpose of this book is to bring together the many management theories, principles, methods and techniques which you can use to help your continuous development. Use it as a management toolbox from which to select the tools to help you manage more effectively. For new managers there may be much to learn. For managers who are more experienced, the development process is about refreshing your knowledge and keeping up to date. This book is a reference which points you in the direction of the inputs on which you will need to draw to achieve or maintain your competence as a manager. Use it by dipping into it to supplement the knowledge and skills you already have and to support your store of decision-making techniques.

Where you identify gaps in your knowledge, undertake to fill them by first referring to your NVQ/SVQ adviser/assessor, mentor and work managers. They will be able to advise you on the most appropriate way to gain the knowledge and skills you need. And, just as important, you should read widely from the range of management books published. The IMI can provide you with a starting point of a recommended reading list, as well as providing details of its own publications. Another rich source of management information on the most up-to-date thinking and practice is journals, including those produced by the IMI which have been researched and written with a focus of management within the motor industry.

This book is about the knowledge and understanding needed by practising managers whose work is at NVQ/SVQ Level 3. MCI defines these people as those with 'a tightly defined area of responsibility for achieving specific results by using resources effectively; responsibility for allocating work to team members, colleagues or contractors'. Whilst the text of this book is a unit and element structure, remember also to refer to MCI's personal competences to help your development.

Always remember, management is a generic activity and the knowledge and skills you have should be transferable to any management situation. Industry-specific knowledge (such as the motor industry) is an added dimension which makes you more effective within your sector. There is no defined format which can be used by all managers. It is your personal competence which will make you an effective manager.

I would like to acknowledge the help and advice given to me by colleagues during the writing of this book, particularly those at MCI who have kept me up to date with progress and changes to the new Management Standards.

PUBLISHER'S INTRODUCTION

This book, while giving a general outline of the subject, has been designed primarily to help in the knowledge and understanding required for National Vocational Qualifications (NVQs) and the Scottish equivalent (SVQs) in Management, Level 3. This series of books does not include Managing Energy or Managing Quality at the moment. Management Charter Initiative (MCI) can provide further information about the knowledge and understanding for these qualifications and units.

NVQs/SVQs are based on national standards required for employment and as such cover all sectors and levels of employment. The assessment of these qualifications is based on a person's ability to show his or her competence against the standards which have been defined. There are no set courses of study or training and the assessment is carried out when the candidate is ready, not when the assessor decrees. There is no pass or failure; the person concerned is either competent or not-yet-competent.

'Competence' means being able to perform the job to the standards expected by employers in the industry. The NVQ/SVQ is broken down into Units of Competence, each of which covers a reasonably self-contained aspect of the occupation. The Units are further sub-divided into Elements of Competence and then into Performance Criteria. It is against the Performance Criteria and Knowledge that the candidate is assessed.

While competence is measured in the actual DOING of the task, there is obviously a need for underlying knowledge which the candidate must have in order to be able to carry out the work involved. This, known in NVQ/SVQ terms as The Underpinning Knowledge, is the subject matter of this book.

To relate the material here to the part of the NVQ/SVQ being covered, there are indicators used. The Unit is used as the chapter heading and sub-headings indicate the Elements. To assist those who select from the book at the time of familiarising themselves with a *specific* Performance Criteria, the Underpinning Knowledge is detailed in that section, with some information perhaps repeated from other Performance Criteria, or a cross-reference is given to the related section or sections.

These Management Vocational Qualifications, formulated by the lead body Management Charter Initiative, are organised in key role areas - **A** units are concerned with Managing Activities; **B** units with Managing Resources; **C** units with Managing People; and **D** units with Managing

Information; there are also the **E** units concerned with managing energy and **F** units with managing quality, mentioned earlier.

The candidate starting on the NVQ/SVQ trail will be informed about the Core Units, the units essential for qualification, and of what choices may be made from the Optional Units. To assist in referencing this volume, each chapter heading indicates whether the Unit being covered is Core or Optional. The Optional Units are indicated by italic entry in the list of Contents which follow.

The Institute of the Motor Industry, publisher of this series of books, is the major awarding body for NVQs/SVQs in the motor industry. The text in this volume, however, is applicable to Management skills in all industries and organisations.

ROY WARD FIMI
Director General,
The Institute of the Motor Industry

Contents

Optional Units in italics

CORE UNIT A1

MAINTAIN ACTIVITIES TO MEET REQUIREMENTS

A1.1 Maintain work activities to meet requirements

Systems surround us in all types of work situations, whether in companies which provide services, or which produce or deliver goods. Maintaining work flow is about designing, using and redesigning *systems* which help you and your work-team carry out your jobs effectively. The concept of systems within management is exactly the same as that within something like a car engine. Many people are probably familiar to some extent with a car engine, where there are inbuilt automatic sensors and comparators which help maintain the desired outputs of speed and fuel efficiency of the engine. Management systems similarly need a logical sequence of activities with opportunities to re-assess and re-evaluate whether they are meeting their purpose.

In your own work you should find you are continuously monitoring what is happening so that you can re-appraise the ways you do things to use resources more efficiently or effectively. Effective monitoring is unobtrusive, but is part of the normal cycle of activity. Complex situations can be assessed relatively easily if you break things down into the simple steps of a basic system of input, process, output. The *output* is the *objective* or *purpose*. The *process* is about how you are going to get the job done, and the *inputs* are who and what you need to do it.

This framework is a good starting point:
- what is your objective? - eg satisfied customer, repaired car, to provide the service at X cost in Y time
- how are you going to get there? - eg what work tasks and resources are needed
- what is the sequence of activities? - eg work plans and schedules
- who are going to do the different jobs? - named individuals for specific activities
- what equipment and/or material is required? - eg parts, computers
- how much will it cost? - eg per activity, per job

Planning is essential. *Objectives* are simply goals which you and your work-team are to achieve. Achieving these may sometimes mean stretching people beyond their past experiences. But, they should still be achievable and realistic, and not impose inappropriate challenges which might simply raise stress levels and even reduce output. Effective management is about helping and *motivating* your work-team to realise their objectives within a framework of tolerance and support.

You will normally be able to make *operational decisions* automatically in accordance with previously agreed responsibilities as they are concerned with daily routine matters which fit in the overall policy framework. Most of these will not require you to make judgements or use discretion; for example routine replenishment of materials.

But, there are times when you will need to solve non-routine problems and take decisions. Immediate problems will need immediate action. Others, such as those that might have arisen from team meetings, may need a more thorough and systematic consideration. Try to put some time aside regularly for this type of situation.

You should find this framework useful:
- *analyse the situation*
    what is the nature of the problem?
    is it technical, financial, personal, a mixture?
    how did it arise?
    is it self-contained, or is it as a result of some other underlying
        cause?
    what is or are the fundamental causes?
- *collect data and information*
- *examine all the facts*
- *plan a solution*
    break down large problems into smaller parts
    prepare a list of resources necessary to implement a successful
        solution
    compare this with resources available
    identify environmental conditions that must remain constant
- *consider all possible solutions*
    list the people who will be involved in the implementation of any
        chosen solution
    ask for views and discuss them with your work-team, other
        colleagues and relevant managers
    identify any barriers that need to be addressed
    outline the best possible solution

You can encourage ownership of work tasks by providing each member of your work-team with their own *job schedule*. This can encourage *ownership* for their own part of the activity and give them a framework within which to work. Make sure each job schedule shows the minimum details of the job to which it refers; the number and type of activities to be carried out; the labour to be used.

In order to make maximum use of equipment, materials and staff, to establish and meet target dates and to improve staff morale, your *master job/work schedule* is your timetable which will help to balance resource requirements against resource availability. The overriding factor is likely to be completion by a given date or time, but there are other considerations when arranging work to minimise costs, such as:

- are you using physical resources to the maximum?
- are you considering storage constraints?
- are you maximising use of staff?
- is your result meeting customers' needs?

How effective is your overall scheduling? A master schedule, which brings together each individual work schedule, will help you to forecast your loading and resource allocations. Do you have all the information you need - for example:

- the dates and/or times when the finished jobs or tasks are due?
- the work schedules for the various jobs or tasks?
- the capacities of your various sections?
- planned maintenance schedules (where equipment is used)?
- planned holidays?
- any anticipated sickness or absenteeism?
- existing commitments?
- availability of resources?
- any external priorities set for individual jobs?
- any allowances for re-work?

Bar charts, whether drawn up manually or on a computer, are effective ways of plotting scheduled activities. Schedules will also help you to be able to consider:

- *costing data* where there is a labour content and services need to be costed
- *dealing with unplanned interruptions to work* such as absence, machinery or equipment breakdowns, etc
- *plant maintenance* where disruptions can be planned
- *manpower planning* for increase or decrease in business volume
- *work balancing* to ensure fair apportionment of work
- *alternative methods* where the final choice will be linked to cost
- *training standards* where a person must work competently

Formal *method study* seeks to simplify work, eliminate unnecessary tasks, and avoid duplication of effort, but this same framework can be used rather more informally to help you look at how efficient or effective the work is for which you are responsible.

- what methods are currently being used?
- what is the purpose of each task?
- who performs each operation?
- where does each job take place?
- when are activities carried out?
- how are they done?
- what are the costs of each individual activity?

Work measurement can be seen as detailed inspection since it is about quantifying the time taken by someone of a certain level of skill to perform a specific task at a predetermined pace of work. But, again, you could use this flexibly and involve those carrying out the work by encouraging them to time themselves and then reach agreement among the team members about what is a realistic time.

Have the *layout* and *physical conditions* of your workplace kept pace with flexible working, multi-skilling, information technology? A great deal of fatigue and stress can be caused inadvertently by the physical environment no longer supporting the nature of the work that is carried on. *Flow charts*, or *process charts*, are useful here.

One of your key responsibilities will be to ensure that daily activities and other initiatives uphold and enhance *quality*. An effective quality-assurance system requires everyone to work together and to share responsibility for quality. Motivate your staff by encouraging them to manage the quality of their own output. This will not only help to reduce inspections but can help to promote a cost-conscious environment.

There are a number of techniques and methods which can be used for monitoring and analysis and which can be used in any management situation, at any level. Effective analysis needs to draw on both *quantitative* and *qualitative* information, with contributions from those who are involved in implementation. The following are some of the ways in which quality might be checked:

- **Inspection**
- **Systematic approaches** such as:
   Pareto analysis - useful for identifying major symptoms
   Cause and effect diagram (Ishikawa diagram) or *fishbone diagram* - useful for mapping the inputs which affect quality

Statistical process control (SPC) - statistical people-based process control procedures

Acceptance sampling - used to decide whether to accept or reject a batch of items

Process capability - a sampling process over a period of time

Quality index

Quality circles

- **Statistical and graphical methods** which are likely to form part of your analysis would be:

A *frequency distribution* - used to tabulate how many times a variable occurs

A *histogram chart*

Normal (or Gaussian) distribution

Mean charts - used when the process over a period is thought to be under control

Range charts used for control of process variability where sample standard deviations can be plotted.

Number defective or *np charts* - used to set warning and action lines

Proportion defective (p) charts used when it is not possible to take samples of constant size

The *Poisson distribution* describes the results obtained from counting defects

Cusum charts are useful for plotting the evolution of processes

Face-to-face communication will probably be the most frequent way you communicate in your work. It has many advantages as you can use *language* appropriate to the listener, you can use *tone, words or body language* to emphasise your meaning, you don't have to worry about spelling and punctuation and other aspects of laying out written work; you can see your impact and get instant *feedback*. Think about how you approach both your spoken and written communications:

- are you always *courteous*?
- do you *listen* to what the other person's response is when received, either verbally or in writing?
- is your *style* appropriate to each situation and the other people?
- do you think about and *plan* your case beforehand?
- do you use appropriate *language* rather than technical jargon as a cover-up for lack of knowledge or to 'fool' the other person?
- do you have mannerisms which are likely to distract your listener in a face-to-face situation?

- do you choose an appropriate time to get your message across - bad timing can frequently sink otherwise good arguments?
- do you *structure* your points logically?
- do you build in aspects you know the other person will find positive?
- have you *defined* the other person's role in relation to your case?

There are circumstances when written material is better, such as *instructions* which have to be followed or which contain *specifications* or complex data; where you may not see the recipient; when something will require referring to *frequently*; when something applies to several members of your work-team; and when it is vital that there is no misunderstanding.

Reports, letters, memoranda, notices, e-mail etc, are all methods of written communications which you are likely to use during the course of your work. Assess your own strengths and weaknesses as a communicator and draw up an action plan of how you intend to overcome your weaknesses.

A1.2   Maintain healthy, safe and productive working conditions

Every year hundreds of fatalities occur and many thousands of people suffer injuries as a direct result of accidents at work. Everyone, from your managing director to the youngest and newest employee, has a part to play in creating and maintaining healthy and safe working conditions.

Every organisation needs an active programme of accident *prevention* within a properly thought-out policy. Safe working practices, systems and procedures must be set up and adhered to. Your task is to promote and maintain a high level of safety consciousness among your work-team and other colleagues and even to those in more senior positions. Safety is not an exciting topic and, in the past, has often been met with indifference or even open hostility, particularly where safety practices may be time-consuming, inconvenient, or might reduce earnings.

Senior managers in companies with more than five people are required to prepare and circulate safety policies for the whole company. You are the 'on-the-spot' manager who is in a position to know whether or not safety arrangements are working in practice. A well-managed organisation should encourage you to be able directly to influence health and safety matters. Help to create a 'total-involvement' approach which stresses the need for the participation of every individual team member. With continuous monitoring, injuries and damage to health can be much reduced. Draw up your own working document, such as a checklist, for your own section/department and use it as a *safety audit* document.

Make sure you know about all the health and safety *legislation* which affects your company as well as all industry *Codes of Practice* and internal *procedures*. Where necessary, provide some training. Encourage discussion within regular team meetings. Remember, your own example is important.

A good starting point is an induction to your company during the first day any new employee begins work. Make sure you include part-time and contractual workers as well as full-time and permanent workers. Make it your responsibility that anyone who is working for you knows about:
- personal responsibilities
- employer responsibilities
- fire or serious accident emergency procedures; alarms, extinguishers, evacuation
- first aid facilities and responsibilities

- reporting procedures
- permitted and prohibited use of equipment
- expected safe behaviour - involving, for example, overalls, foot-wear, loose clothing, long hair, watches, rings, ties, use of chemicals, inflammable substances, acids, fumes, electricity, skin care, machinery driving
- safe methods of working, including using guards on machinery
- safe storage and disposal of waste
- safe ways of conducting oneself
- hygiene and cleanliness rules

Sometimes, unfortunately, accidents do happen. Learn from them. Make a report. The headings could be what actually happened - the damage resulting; the injuries sustained; the action taken at the time; how the department kept working until full repairs were completed; the cause; recommendations to prevent a recurrence.

Despite an intention in the Health and Safety at Work Act 1974 to include safeguards to mental as well as physical aspects of health, to date very little attention has been given to the mental aspects of health. A customer-driven culture, together with high-speed manipulation of data via computers, is driving change at an ever-quickening pace. Managers need to become involved in identifying *stress* that can result from all this, and manage and help to prevent the negative face of it.

Normal stress can help people work better and more effectively. It becomes a problem when employees and their performance begin to suffer as a result. Obviously there are factors outside work which can make the situation worse for people, such as racial or sexist prejudice, family problems, and so on. But, as the work environment is more likely to be controllable than outside factors, it seems logical to attempt to tackle sources of stress at work.

Understanding the causes of stress will help you to use it constructively in the work environment. As a manager you are in part responsible for the environment in which your team work and you can help in reducing the harmful effects of stress on the people who work for you. Can you do anything to reduce stress levels where it is causing problems?

This framework may be a good starting point:
- *environmental* - these factors, for example, might be considered: high levels of noise; poor lighting or ventilation; overcrowding; vibration; incorrect temperatures; toxic fumes and chemicals; badly-designed furniture; open-plan offices; poor maintenance; poor rest facilities; no child-care facilities.

- *job design* - work factors to be considered might include: repetitious and boring aspects; too much or too little of it; poor pace and flow; too much or too little supervision; lack of direction and decision-making; constant sitting or constant standing; lack of adequate rest breaks; working uncomfortably with machinery or VDUs; lack of job control; under-utilisation of skills; unexpected and unexplained change.
- *contractual* - low pay; unsocial hours; shift work; excessive hours of overtime; flexitime; job insecurity (including short term and temporary contracts).
- *relationships* - bad relationships with supervisors or team; sexism/racism/ageism (including harassment and discrimination); a high level of customer or client complaints; impersonal treatment at work; lack of communication; lack of control; autocratic management styles.

The big issue to get across is that health and safety is everyone's responsibility.

A1.3 Make recommendations for improvements to work activities

The process of setting *operational objectives* within the framework of your company's *corporate strategy* is essentially a system of measuring and comparing performance against a defined target. It should be a formal process and one in which all members of your company should become involved at some point within their work-team.

It provides opportunities for focusing on those aspects of work for which managers like you have responsibility and encourages team members to make an effective contribution to planning and carrying out their work. Most organisations carry out an annual review to see what progress they have made with their current objectives during the year.

But business is not static, and initiatives and projects which augment the overall plans are likely during the year. Objectives and *action plans*, with dates, costs, specific targets and detailed work allocations, need to support those activities.

Implementing plans effectively means first making them known to those who will be involved in carrying them through or to others who might be affected by them. It is more likely you will reach a realistic and workable plan in which they are to support and carry it out if you encourage their input.

Be systematic and establish objectives which are achievable, realistic and measurable - ie you will know when you have attained what you set out to do. Define how objectives are to be met, eg by deciding methods of work and establishing who is responsible for achieving the objectives; state by when they are to be achieved; quantify, both financially and numerically.

Develop your system by building in the measures against which achievement can be *monitored*. Pre-scheduled regular meetings or informal team meetings to *monitor* and review progress will help keep you on track. The purpose is to measure how much of the objectives have been achieved and to define any new ones for the next period in the light of the outcomes.

This process can also provide you with a good opportunity to review *performance* by individuals. Team and personal development objectives can be defined around this same programme of work in exactly the same way. Whether you have a formal appraisal system or more informal arrangements for agreeing personal development opportunities with your work-team, you can define and agree measures which can be achieved and reviewed from time to time.

Evaluating the effectiveness of particular aspects of work is probably something you will do periodically, or at regular and planned opportunities. Hopefully you have a *participatory* management style and prompts for mechanical changes, such as designing new forms for revised procedures or improving the system for receiving keys where a customer leaves a car for service, are likely to arise from within your work-team itself. You could even be responsible for initiating change in the first place, having recognised improvements as a result of regular monitoring within your own section or department.

But whichever is the case, you will be involved in selling the changes, introducing them and implementing them within your own work group. Large-scale changes will usually involve more senior managers becoming involved to deal with overall arrangements, particularly where changes are going to affect several parts of your organisation.

Where you do identify improvements that can be made, such as to a job, procedures, ways of working etc, you need to convince those around you of the benefits and improvements they will bring. Sometimes this is no easy task.

But you can make a convincing case by preparing it in a well-researched and structured way. Try combining the systems framework in element A1.1 with this one:

- What is the precise nature of the recommended change(s)?
- Why is it necessary?
- What's wrong with what happens now?
- Can it be justified?
- What will be the advantages, compared with the present situation, and from whose point of view?
- What will be the benefits for others?
- What will be the benefits for you?
- What will be the particular benefits for your team?
- What other positive spin-offs might also be achieved?
- When would you intend to make the changes?
- Over what time-scale?
- Are you sure you aren't trying to push things through too quickly?
- Will the groundwork have been completed effectively?
- Will people be ready for the change when it happens?
- Who is likely to feel threatened?

- Who is involved?
- When will they need to be informed?
- What would be their involvement?

When you get to the point of putting your proposals forward, make sure you give yourself the best chance of having them accepted by presenting them in an appropriate way. It might be through a verbal discussion or meeting, a formal presentation, a written report, or simply a notice on the board.

The means must fit the context. If you work for a large company it is quite likely there is an established way of doing this type of thing and you should familiarise yourself with it. If you are in a much smaller company, it might be a more informal approach. But, where there is a certain amount of detail which others need to consider and remember, it is usual to have some form of written communication.

Planning is the key for success when you need to present formal recommendations. You may find this framework useful:

Prepare
have you got all the facts and can you support them?
what objections might be raised to your ideas?
can you refute them?
have you presented all your supporting materials such as costs, duty roster, etc, in an easily understandable way?
are you sure you have considered all aspects of your plan?
have you highlighted sufficiently the benefits to your company which could arise from adopting your ideas?
have you prepared how and what you will say, and made notes to help you?

Present your proposals
get to the point quickly
explain why you are taking this course of action or making these proposals
show any alternatives you have considered and why you have ruled them out
finally, summarise your argument and don't forget to show the cost and stress the benefits

Handling questions
be prepared to answer questions, as this shows your listeners are interested in what you have said

deal with all questions politely and don't feel goaded by criticisms - these can also be positive to your proposals

where objections are made, try to show how your proposals can overcome them

Whether you are putting proposals forward to your work-team, senior managers, clients, suppliers or customers, your self-presentation can be just as important as what you have to say. Pay attention to how you will project yourself in a way that is equally positive with your proposals.

CORE UNIT B1

SUPPORT THE EFFICIENT USE OF RESOURCES

B1.1 Make recommendations for the use of resources

As a unit leader you will be responsible for setting objectives for your work-team's activities and the structure of your company will determine what the 'unit' is for setting them. A pure *functional* form, where people are grouped according to their similarities in terms of activity or expertise, eg new sales, repair, is probably the most common. A *project* approach is often adequate for a very small company and is being increasingly used in larger organisations to provide a flexible workforce and multi-disciplinary teams, thus giving a *matrix* structure which arrays across functional boundaries.

Planning is deciding what to do in the future. It may take some time but it forces you to clarify your *objectives*, plan *targets* and design ways of achieving them, and to develop *monitoring measures, processes* and *procedures*. Some things you can predict with a reasonable amount of certainty, others you cannot. But you can make *contingency plans* for things that might occur. All organisations need to keep improving and changing their ways of working if they are to survive and continue to satisfy their customers' requirements. A company with ways of working that could be very much improved will need to examine its processes and the resources used. It will need to plan and find new ways of meeting its customers' needs. This will include making sure that it has sufficient money to carry those plans through. New ways of working nearly always require additional or a different mix of resources.

Your resource requirements - people, materials, finance, time, energy, services, equipment - need to be balanced against what is available. Different work methods can be used for different types of activity. For example, your main business might be car service and repair and you will do this on a *job basis*; paying suppliers may be on a *batch* basis when it is carried out once a month. Your organisation's structure should reflect the type of work methods which you use daily. You need to understand your daily business well in order to plan and sequence activities effectively. Many organisations are now '*customer driven*' - whether in manufacturing or provision of services and this can pose problems of peaks and troughs in demand which you will need to manage effectively. If you look at your own situation:

- how much work can you deal with by using existing resources?
- what would be the effect if you made changes to your resources?
- how do you cope with peaks and troughs?
- what effect would changes in work methods produce?
- when do you need to change the amount of resources to cope with increases or decreases in jobs?

A *departmental/section/unit plan* which supports your company's overall strategy is useful for both yourself and staff alike. When you are drawing one up, it will help you to focus on such things as important areas for development, changes that are going to be made, targets that need to be achieved. It will help you to identify whether you have all the resources, equipment and skills that are needed to carry the plan through. If you consider alternative courses of action, it will help you to *evaluate* the consequences of each and choose the most suitable. And it will provide you with good opportunities to *motivate* members of your work-team by involving them in specifying and agreeing targets.

Your own manager will probably call upon you to provide operational data at the annual budget-setting time, when you will have an opportunity to re-examine how costs are incurred. Two ways you can influence costs are either by increasing productivity or reducing basic costs.

The use of information from regular monitoring of routine work activities will help you in *planning* your future work. Some useful techniques to help are shown in B1.2. Also, *network analysis* or *critical path analysis* (CPA) is a powerful technique which will help you to plan and schedule activities, whether you do this manually or on a computer. There are also some good computer PERT packages on the market which take optimistic, pessimistic and most-likely views. *Loading* and *scheduling* exercises will help you to plan more effective use of resources and to ensure they are to hand when needed. Consider questions such as:

- Does the *layout* of your premises, equipment and work stations still make sense and enable resources to be used efficiently? For example, how much time is wasted moving unnecessary distances between where work is carried out and where materials are stored?
- Do people who need to work together frequently have to keep getting up and moving to another location?

15

- Is information kept conveniently close to those who are using it regularly?

Sometimes these things can be improved by the use of computers and electronics; others need more traditional approaches.

But being a manager is not just about developing the ability to identify opportunities for improvement. It is also about being able to contribute to the cost-justification of ideas. Just as with being required to justify existing expenditure within current budgets, you will need to be able to produce good cost/benefit arguments for changes and new developments. *Cost benefit analysis* is a useful technique to help you here. Your plans need to be accompanied by a draft budget, which will give some indication of the anticipated expenditure, as this will give both your managers and you a reasonable idea of what costs need to be budgeted for during the forthcoming financial period. Cost justification involves outlining the costs and benefits so as to highlight the effects that implementing your proposals will have on your company's finances. Draft your ideas out carefully to get the ball rolling and work with your manager on more detailed figures on forecasts and likely increases or decreases in costs.

Forecasting is an essential prerequisite to effective planning but, in management, predictions are sometimes difficult to achieve since they are based on experience of the past and there is no guarantee that past trends or environments will continue. However, short-term predictions are likely to be easier to make and be nearer the mark than long-term ones which are undertaken by senior management. One of the most important of all business forecasts is that of future 'sales' whether of services or products. Finance is needed to bridge the gap between expenditure on inputs that is incurred now and income that is not received until sales have been made. Forecasts of increased volume - or, alternatively, reduced volume - will obviously have implications for your *work capacity, loading* and *work scheduling, physical resources*, as well as the numbers of *people employed* with particular skills. You will need to use statistical methods such as *probability* and *normal* and *Poisson distributions. Sampling distributions, time series* graphs and *tests of significance* will also help you with forecasting. You are probably already familiar with the methods from which you can choose when making a case in writing, such as memos, letters, reports, notices, manuals, forms, etc. You should select the most appropriate according to your needs at the time. You will normally find most of your written communications are internal, so this should make it easier to judge the *style* and *tone* you should use.

Remember, your manager is unlikely to know all the intricate details of your day-to-day activities, whilst your work-team will be very familiar with them. Consequently, you should ensure you apply the appropriate amount of *detail* according to whom you are trying to reach.

If you have to prepare a case to support your plans, you will need to plan your information thoroughly beforehand. This framework should help you to prepare a report or a presentation:

- a *heading* that identifies your proposal clearly, together with your name and section or department, date and any time-scale that is needed for a decision to be made
- a **very** brief *summary* of what you want, how much it costs, and the key benefits
- an *introduction* which brings your reader or listener up-to-speed with the situation; you could include such things as any problems which brought you to this point, how work is currently carried out and why changes are needed; why a new piece of equipment is required
- the *solution* which makes clear exactly what your proposals will mean to your section or department
- the *justification* of the costs and benefits which would be achieved by your recommendations; include any impact on profits, cash and assets; show time-scales
- make *forecasts* and *estimates* within a realistic range and include supporting evidence to justify the figures you use
- show *time-scales* within which the cost or benefit is most likely to occur - usually within three time windows of: immediate, this financial year, later
- show a *credibility check* where you have consulted relevant managers and financial advisers
- provide detailed number and financial *calculations* in an appendix which can be analysed or questioned when your recommendations are being considered
- reiterate your recommendations and make your *conclusions*; emphasise the strongest reasons for supporting your ideas
- have you got all the facts and can you support them?

If you are invited to put your ideas forward verbally you should get to the point quickly and explain why you are making these proposals. Show the alternatives that you have considered and why you have ruled them out. Do not forget to point out the disadvantages, but highlight the advantages. Finally, summarise your case; don't forget to show the costs, and also stress the benefits. You are likely to be asked questions so be prepared to answer them as this shows your listeners are interested in what you have said. Deal with them politely and don't feel goaded by criticisms; these are not automatically negative but can be highly constructive and even augment your own proposals. Where objections are made, try to show how your proposals can overcome them. Some of these questions might help you to prepare and review your case:

- what objections might be raised to your ideas?
- can you refute them?
- have you included all your supporting material, such as costs, duty rosters, etc in an easily understandable way?
- are you sure you have considered all aspects of your plan?
- have you highlighted sufficiently the benefits to your company of adopting your ideas?
- have you prepared what you will say and how, and made notes to help you?

B1.2 Contribute to the control of resources

A supervisory manager's section/department begins to cost money as soon as the day's work begins. Budgets are part of the planning ahead process; in fact, they are *plans* expressed in financial terms. Your knowledge of day-to-day activities in your section or department is vital to setting realistic targets for output and/or performance. Your budget should help you to ensure that the finances for which you are responsible are properly *controlled* so that your company will survive and prosper. It will help you to *co-ordinate* the spending needs of the different activities without one part running ahead of the others. It will provide you with opportunities to *communicate* and *motivate* your work-team by involving them in the annual budget-setting cycle. It will help you to *compare* actual results with predictions. Although a budget is built around historic data to some extent, there should be a meaningful allocation for development and achieving new *objectives* which move your section or unit forward.

Drawing up your budget means you need to establish how your section/ department costs are incurred by defining *cost centres* to which *expenditure* can be allocated. Then you need to distinguish between *direct expenditures* such as wages, and *indirect costs* such as heating and other types of *overheads*. Compiling a budget which is realistic and achievable needs your work-team and other colleagues to be motivated towards working with it. Their input in its planning will help to promote ownership and the end result it likely to be more acceptable than a budget which is enforced and used as a kind of strait-jacket. Build in scope for realistic development and reasonable new initiatives. Consult and inform your work-team and managers about your proposals and encourage constructive ideas.

Without some kind of *monitoring* and *control* it is all too easy for staff unthinkingly to use more resources than are actually required. The process of monitoring usage should be an active part of everyday working life and not appear as a kind of inspection where staff may feel threatened. Monitoring the accuracy of events as they occur and comparing them with errors will help you when checking how close the predictions are to reality. The outcomes from this will provide accurate records which you can use for subsequent planning activities. Other types of monitoring are usually to do with the use of resources and supplies. Whether you hold stock, or use a *JIT* system and use manual or computerised information systems, accurate records need to be kept. Here are useful methods for collecting facts and recording physical work:

- *process charts* - useful to portray a sequence of events diagramatically
- *string diagrams* - useful to show movement between workstations and compare values of different layouts

and two methods for recording information flow:

- *procedure charts* - useful means of recording detailed and complicated data which normally constitute a procedure
- *systems analysis* - normally computer programs which can manipulate extensive data

The efficiency measures and variances you are likely to be concerned with will be along the lines of volume variance, price variance, usage variance, yield variance, materials mix variance, scrap/wastage variance, utilisation variance, efficiency variance. Effectiveness is about comparing whether you have met the *standard* or *benchmark* that has been set.

Value analysis is a useful technique which you can use to examine where costs are incurred. Reducing costs depends on observation and common sense, keeping records, and measuring performance against standards which have been set. Look at your work-team and make sure you use the right person for the task; part-time or sub-contracted staff may be more cost effective; provide training as necessary; give clear instructions; and find ways to motivate them. Use materials which are right for the job - no better, no worse. Order any materials in usable quantities and don't have unnecessary surplus; control the flow of materials; store materials safely and correctly so wastage isn't incurred, including theft; look at re-use or scrap policies. If equipment is used, make sure each person is trained to use it correctly; plan regular maintenance so that it doesn't break down and waste time; monitor any equipment faults and you will be able to detect any trends arising. Keep records which are simple, clear, easy to maintain up-to-date, and available.

You should be constantly seeking to ensure your section or department is operating efficiently and that costs incurred are not excessive and are within agreed budget. Try to foster morale improvement through better use of time. You can use some of the time and work analysis techniques shown in Unit A1, but it is important you brief your work-team members to encourage their support and to alleviate any concerns they may have or any feelings of 'inspection':

- *work measurement* - used to measure the time taken to carry out an activity or task

- *time study* - used for recording times and rates of working for an element of a specified task
- *synthesis* - used to build up the time for a task at a defined level of performance
- *activity sampling* - conducted over a period of time to measure the percentage of time an activity occurs

Be reasonable in your approach, since excessive short-run cost-cutting can lead to much greater inefficiencies over the longer term. Effective cost control depends as much on an appropriate frame of mind as on specific measures. Schemes which originate within your work-team and in which team members are involved are more likely to be effective than those that are simply imposed. Many organisations which operate with a *participatory* management style are finding benefits by agreeing levels of responsibility for operating resource controls within work-teams themselves. Try and foster a spirit of trust to promote *motivation* and encourage systems which are routine and in which staff take responsibility for ensuring that their own work uses optimum resources. This framework may be useful to examine your systems:

- are your records accurate and can you identify such things as excessive use of consumables, or costs to overheads, over-maintenance, scrap?
- have you examined work practices to see if there are better ways to do things and which could be less costly?
- are your work-team appropriately trained to carry out their work, especially where costs are being incurred through re-work or it is taking longer than it should to complete a job?
- are safety rules being followed: if not, are people using unsafe equipment which may result in lost time through accidents, or creating idle equipment which cannot be used?
- do you re-use or re-cycle where possible?
- do you insist on good housekeeping, such as using time switches for heating?
- do you keep a watch on staff using time and resources which are not company work?

A system which ensures stock movements are recorded at the same time as the work is undertaken will help with aspects of your monitoring and control, particularly in ensuring there is little or no wastage; eradicating 'shrinkage' (theft); recognising inadequate quality of materials; ensuring resources are delivered on time. Help your staff to understand how important this task is and encourage them to be systematic in recording all stock movements accurately and timely. Whether you have a manual or computerised system records need to be kept on:

- all replenishments and withdrawals
- different stock types - eg work-in-progress, parts, etc
- issuance dates and replenishment dates
- the selling price (to either an internal cost centre or an external customer)
- the cost of purchase
- the job for which the stock has been used

If you keep this data with your job schedules you will be able to use it to help you make sensible forecasts and plan future activities such as resourcing requirements and costs of future jobs. Use it also to assess how effectively your section is keeping to budget - either periodically or on a per-job basis. If you need to implement *cost reduction* programmes you should relate them to specific activities rather than apply a vague objective of cutting total costs by 5% during a year. Careful planning and detailed records of successes or failures must be kept and all programmes carried through. Spreading the responsibility for cutting costs among named people will help to create greater cost awareness.

CORE UNIT C1

MANAGE YOURSELF

C1.1 Develop your own skills to improve your performance

Personal development must go hand-in-hand with business development, otherwise your company will be unable to achieve the goals it has set. There has been a considerable amount of research work undertaken to try and understand how individuals function and equally as much work on attempting to understand how organisations function. It is worthwhile being aware of the major theories and principles which have resulted as it will help you to understand how people relate to and interact with each other, as well as enhancing your skills to be an effective and competent manager.

To get the best from your staff, you need to have regard for the needs of individuals, and facilitate motivation by generating a spirit of involvement and co-operation. Thus, your management style is critical to the success of your role as a manager leader. Which of these styles portrays you - *authoritarian, paternalistic, democratic, laissez-faire?* Studies appear to support the claim that there is no single behaviour category of leadership which is superior; the effectiveness depends upon the variables of the particular situation.

If you are registered with an awarding body as a candidate on an NVQ/SVQ Management programme, you will have been provided with a portfolio of documents to help you with your development. Begin with the self-analysis, which will help you get a base for your personal development plan. Focus your mind on your goals and start to set the scene for planning how you are going to achieve them. Talk it over with your manager and/or mentor and with your NVQ/SVQ programme adviser or assessor. These questions might help you to get started:
- what information do you need and how are you going to get it?
- who are going to be the most likely people who can help you?
- what needs to be done and when?
- what can you do on a day-to-day basis?
- are there any tasks which need to be done before others?
- are there any obstacles likely to prevent you from achieving any of your goals?

- what personal learning do you think you are likely to need?
- what are the likely positive and negative consequences for achieving your goals?
- how will people around you be affected?
- are there any cost implications and how will you manage them?
- how will achieving these goals help you to achieve other goals?
- what is important to you about achieving each of these goals?
- how will you reward yourself along the way?
- what will achieving all this you?

Even if you think you are already a good manager, you are recommended to follow the self-analysis. You can construct a personal development plan quite easily by using the element titles and performance criteria from the MCI Management Standards if you are not an NVQ or SVQ candidate. If you use the framework of the Management Standards, together with their model for Personal Competence, you will find it provides you with a coherent approach which can be integrated quite easily into work objectives or performance review systems. If you meet regularly with your manager or mentor they can help you to *monitor* and *review* your progress to keep on track, just in the same way you would review the *performance* of your work-team members.

When you have achieved your goals, take some time to reflect on everything that has happened and what you have learned. You can use the *storyboard* approach to justify your evidence and to suggest how you would do something differently or better if you were to undertake that activity again. *Reflective analysis* is an important part of personal development and the sort of questions you could ask yourself are:
- what have you learned and gained from your experience?
- how have you changed?
- what problems did you encounter and how did you resolve them?
- what can you learn from them and how can you use this experience to prevent similar problems in the future?
- what are you capable of now that you weren't previously?
- with the benefit of hindsight, what would you have done differently and how can you use this knowledge in the future?

There are many books on management around, some of which are based on in-depth academic research and others which offer lighter reading and 'quick-fix' tips. Use them as tools, dip into them for reference or to update yourself, sift through the concepts and theories and weigh the merits of one against the other, learn how to apply sound principles to your unique situation. Different approaches may suit your own style and that of your company better than others. However, your personal development should include a re-examination of your beliefs as a consideration of whether you are being an effective manager. Developing personal competence means having a willingness to learn and change yourself, as well as the activities being carried out around you.

C1.2 Manage your time to meet your objectives

Management is an integrating activity which permeates right through an organisation, and your management competence is fundamental to day-to-day activities. Management is also about getting things done through people, and, although there is a close relationship between management and *leadership*, the two are not necessarily synonymous, and it does not follow that every manager is a leader. Consequently it is essential that every manager understands the nature of leadership and what makes an effective leader.

Management By Objectives (MBO) is essentially a system or style of management based on the relationship of goals and objectives for the company, integrated into a system of planning in which individuals are involved in setting these objectives and targets for their own work area. For managers, it has the attraction of encouraging a *participatory style* of management and it provides opportunities for staff to accept greater responsibility for their own targets and achievements. The objective-setting process is essentially a system of measuring and comparing performance against a defined target and this helps managers to focus on those aspects of work for which they have responsibility and to encourage team members to make an effective contribution in planning and carrying out their work. Work planning is essential and *objectives* are simply goals which you and your work-team are to achieve.

Short-term, medium-term and long-term objectives need to be prioritised and scheduled in ways which *optimise* time, people and cost. *Operational objectives* are about planning and setting targets which you and your work-team need to achieve within a defined time-scale. Monthly, half-yearly, or yearly objectives might focus on areas which need development, and achieving these may sometimes mean stretching people beyond their past experiences. But they should still be achievable and realistic, and not impose inappropriate challenges which might simply raise stress levels and even reduce output. For regular and routine activities, most managers will need a *master job schedule* which sets out how the team's work is to be organised and carried out. You can encourage each member of your work-team to contribute their own *job schedule* by providing this framework within which they can work. You might find Unit A1 has some useful information.

Effective management is also about helping and *motivating* your work-team to realise their objectives within a framework of tolerance and support. Whilst objectives encourage participation, there is an element of 'scientific management' whereby measurement of achievement of targets is made. Consequently, the way in which you use the process needs to be such that staff are not alienated or turned off, particularly if it is part of an appraisal scheme. The best work systems are only effective if the people involved in using them are *motivated* to achieve optimum results. Ensure you have a reasonable grasp of the complex issues surrounding motivation and the many variables which can influence it. Your ability to maintain motivation within your staff is one of the most complex aspects of management. Recent analysis of 'industrial trends' shows *knowledge workers* to be the core of many sectors of work and managing them effectively is crucial for many organisations. Managers need to move away from the more prescriptive formulas developed for process-driven organisations and embrace a more project or task-based approach to management. The success of knowledge-based work is not dependent on how closely these staff are managed, but how effectively a manager such as yourself can get the staff to manage themselves.

Team and personal development objectives should be linked together around programmes of work. Whether you have a formal appraisal system or more informal arrangements for agreeing personal development opportunities with your work-team, you can define and agree measures which can be achieved and reviewed from time to time. Your *personal goals* need to enable you to achieve team objectives and provide you with challenges for personal development. Once you have defined what they are, you need to plan them in just the same way. Mapping your own individual objectives to the Management Standards will help you to get a clear description of what you are expected to do and how you are going to do it.

If you feel there just isn't enough time in the day to get everything done, it might be that the amount of work really is for at least two people or, as is more often the case, it is just that you need to manage the time you do have better. Some simple guidelines could make all the difference - learn how to delegate; control interruptions; use a daily plan; set objectives; handle each piece of paper only once; train staff better; prioritise tasks; learn to say no; learn to speed read. It is well worth the effort of putting a little time aside at the beginning or end of each day to plan how you will spend your time. Start now.

CORE UNIT C4

CREATE EFFECTIVE WORKING RELATIONSHIPS

C4.1   Gain the trust and support of colleagues and team members

It is difficult to define what an organisation's climate is, but generally it is about the state of mutual trust and understanding between employees. A healthy climate is likely to be expressed by a sense of commitment both by and towards employees. It only exists when an organisation has a viable 'people strategy' that really does unlock individual potential. An unhealthy climate is likely to be littered with destructive conflicts and often poor management. Sustaining high morale and optimism in today's business climate can be hard. The survivors of redundancy programmes are frequently disillusioned, bitter and over-worked. An organisation whose people look alive, are creative and have a sense of well-being is not something that can be bought.

Although the words 'group' and 'team' are often used interchangeably, there is a distinction in that a group is 'any number of people who interact with one another, are psychologically aware of one another, and perceive themselves to be a group'. A team is 'a group of people who have shared goals, share responsibility for the tasks for which it is accountable, and produce an outcome that is greater than the sum of its parts'. To be an effective *work-team* there needs to be a transition from group to team - a process which requires your skills and competence as a manager. The ability of everyone to work together with mutual respect is essential to the evolution of a new culture.

Self-awareness and an ability to analyse relationships will help you to be sensitive to the needs of others and to support them. Your management style is critical to successful relationships with your staff. A number of factors have combined to create resistance against autocratic styles of leadership, including changes in society's value system and broader standards of education. Your style needs to reflect the 1990s. Finding the right time and place to relate to those you see frequently and those with whom you come into contact less frequently needs to be appropriately planned or ad hoc. Generating trust and commitment needs tenacity and constant attention. The pressures of business life in the 1990s can be competitive and stressful. Taking time to build social and non-social relationships with work colleagues can pay dividends in the future. Working on projects across the company can promote better understanding of each other's work problems and constraints. Sharing success can often achieve greater benefits than personal gain. Communication can sometimes be difficult, but learn to develop your inter-personal skills across a range of situations. There are a number of things you can do as a manager to help your work-team:

- be loyal
- find an acceptable balance between being *employee-centred* and *task-centred*
- show concern for safety, health and welfare
- meet individual's needs
- manage team development

It is important formally to build in time during work schedules to exchange views and ideas. Whilst it may be appropriate to hold a formal meeting with a pre-determined agenda, it is also acceptable to use, in appropriate situations, rather more informal ways of exchanging ideas and views. The more supportive your company's cultural system, the easier you will find it to encourage your staff to participate. With a more directive and dictatorial approach you are likely to have more difficulty in generating trust and responsibility for work. Consequently, your management approach must take account not only of the need to have *systems*, but also of the *human and social factors* as well.

With recession and the development of more demanding approaches to management of the workforce, increasing numbers of employees have all too frequently been the butt of unfair practices. Aggressive and unreasonable behaviour at work is not just plain bad management, it is also bad for business. Whilst there has been considerable debate about the issue of equal opportunities, every manager needs to ensure company procedures operate which ensure compliance with legislation covering this area. Everyone has a responsibility to ensure they conduct themselves in a way which does not discriminate unfairly against any other employee or customer. Managers and supervisors carry a special responsibility by virtue of their authority over others. They may recognise that unfair treatment is taking place or have this brought to their attention. In which case they have a responsibility to ensure that swift and appropriate action is taken. Being unaware that such treatment is taking place does not exempt a company from responsibility. Even if managers do not know of such cases it is still possible for your company to be held responsible. It is particularly important to ensure that effective systems are in place to prevent unfair discrimination from occurring and to ensure that any such cases arising are dealt with promptly and effectively and that appropriate follow-up action is taken. In effect, managing and taking decisions which affect other people places managers under an obligation to set a good example and to ensure that their own comments, directives and actions do not condone, contribute to, cause or themselves constitute unfair discrimination. Two pieces of legislation which impinge on equal opportunities, harassment and bullying are the Race Relations Act and the Sex Discrimination Act, plus Codes of Practice covering equal treatment. If someone suffers a detriment or intimidation as a result of their race or sex, they can make a claim under these Acts. Examine your own behaviour to ensure that you are not unwittingly bullying or harassing members of your staff. Learn to recognise any signs shown by any of your colleagues.

Although there is no such thing as perfection in communication, it is something everyone has to work at. The more easily work group members can communicate freely with each other, the more likelihood of group cohesion. The structuring of activities can contribute significantly to the effectiveness of resolving problems and generation of ideas. A *management style* which encourages *participation* in planning and decision-making is more often than not a better *motivator* than an *autocratic authoritarian* approach. That is not to say, however, that you should shirk from communicating unfavourable decisions, only that these will be better understood and more likely to be acceptable. *Consultation* is about generating involvement; informing is about advising your decision. Where you have part-time, temporary or other sub-contracted staff working for you, you will need to consider additional mechanisms of helping integration with your more permanent staff. Their level of interaction is determined by how communication channels are structured. Look at the interaction of your own workforce in the light of the *communication networks* in Unit C12.

By providing your staff with support and interaction there is a greater likelihood you will become an effective work-team. However, there is no panacea for either achieving or maintaining their trust, but you can practice consideration and tolerance within the structure of ensuring work objectives are achieved. In many ways your role will often make you the first line of contact. If staff feel able to contribute and discuss problems with you without feeling threatened or weak you will be going a long way to supplying the necessary support to minimise stress. Being busy often gets in the way and someone who is stressed and anxious may have difficulty either in plucking up the courage to speak to you about the problem or in articulating the problem, or both. Listening to what people have to say involves both eyes and ears. Very often someone can say one thing but mean another. Unless they are very skilled at keeping their emotions hidden, it is usually possible to discern their real meaning by observing body language as well as hearing the words they are saying. Listening is an active skill which involves attention, learning and understanding.

Maintaining the trust of all your colleagues and staff and enabling them to contribute to a successful business means looking for ways to improve personal relationships. Be proactive in building relationships and don't leave them to chance.

C4.2   Gain the trust and support of your manager

Do you manage upwards effectively? The way you perform in your own job is most likely influenced by your own manager's behaviour and style. Most people go to work with the original intention of being eager to do a good job and performing to the best of their abilities. But sometimes the ideal doesn't exist in reality and failure to perform is often the result of how staff perceive they are being treated by their managers. You need to have good interpersonal skills and will certainly need to be able to negotiate effectively if you are to gain commitment to your ideas and plans. All managers need to be politically aware and you should learn how to identify coalitions and balance conflicting goals and perceptions. Try to stand back from your own role and take a helicopter perspective just as your own manager's role does.

There are times when you might disagree with your managers, and it can be difficult to tell them tactfully how you feel. Whatever you decide to say, the first rule is to say it in private. No one likes to be criticised in front of other people. Try to put your objections in the form of questions. Begin by agreeing with the parts you are able to, then ask questions such as what led to the decisions that were made, or what would happen if things went wrong. Let your managers see you have genuine concerns rather than petty arguments. Devise an alternative plan beforehand and put forward a positive proposal to show you have thought things through. If you can come to a satisfactory agreement on the major issues, don't make an issue out of minor points. And, if you find you are in the wrong, don't be afraid to admit it. All you have done is show you are taking your work seriously. If you were misled by having wrong information, explain that was the case, and apologise for your error.

If you have studied group and leadership behaviours you will be in a position to understand work relationships better than someone who has not been introduced to these concepts. Use your own personal development and knowledge to enhance and improve the behaviour and performance of your managers. Just as you would with your own work-team, be willing to look at things from their perspectives and consider alternatives which are put forward objectively. Encourage discussion and participation with a view to increasing each other's understanding and co-operation. Work towards becoming an effective team with your manager where each of you has a positive role and within which each of you can bring different knowledge, skills, and experience.

C4.3   Minimise conflict in your team

Tension and conflict are inevitable features of working life, given the limitations of resources and the often competing needs of individuals and their objectives. Properly managed, however, conflict can be a trigger to improved policies and processes to satisfy both organisational requirements and individual needs. Left to fester, conflict can have detrimental consequences for all concerned. Conflict is a result of obstructing the achievement of goals or needs - either for an individual, a work group, or the company as a whole. It is well worth knowing the potential sources of conflict before they arise so that you will be better able to make contingency plans. At the individual level, however, this can be difficult and, indeed, almost impossible to predict, given the nature of human behaviour. Therefore, the strategies you adopt to minimise harmful effects will vary according to the source of the conflict.

Failure to delegate tasks successfully could mean you are not taking full advantage of the skills of your team members and this could be a cause of conflict. It could also be a potential source of work stress. *Role structure* and differentiation is as important to effective performance of work groups as is *role expectations*. Inadequate or inappropriate role definition can result in *role conflict* - including *role incompatibility, role ambiguity, role overload* and *role underload*. It is important you should make every effort to minimise role conflict and the resultant consequences of role stress. Successful delegation will be affected by both your formal and informal structures, and by whether they have the rigidity of mechanistic systems or are more fluid organic systems.

Getting to the root cause of conflicts is often difficult and it may be a symptom of a quite different problem from the one seemingly apparent. This framework can be useful in identifying possible causes:
- is there a difference in perception between one person and another?
- are different people competing for limited resources?
- is there a likelihood that one person will concentrate on achieving their own objectives when reality requires that another's objectives take precedence?
- is there a likelihood the interdependence of work activities could cause conflict?
- how great is the potential for role conflict?
- are there pressures external to the work-team which, if left unmanaged, could result in conflict?

- are there powerful coalitions which can cause conflict if left to multiply unchecked?
- is there a possibility for staff to feel there is inequality of treatment with their colleagues?

Above all, you need to ensure you talk with and listen to your team members and provide them with opportunities to raise and discuss problems. If they feel able to contribute and discuss problems with you, without feeling threatened or weak, you will be going a long way to supplying the necessary support to minimise stress. Being busy often gets in the way and someone who is stressed and anxious may have difficulty either in plucking up the courage to speak to you about the problem or in articulating the problem, or both. Listening to what people have to say involves both eyes and ears. Very often someone can say one thing but mean another. Unless they are very skilled at keeping their emotions hidden it is usually possible to discern their real meaning by observing body language as well as hearing the words they are saying. Listening is an active skill which involves attention, learning and understanding. You may find some of these strategies useful:

- clarify personal goals and work objectives, and seek to promote those shared by all
- attempt to allocate resources fairly; build in flexibility where possible
- be supportive and adopt a more participatory management style
- examine structures and work activities to see if there are better ways of achieving group cohesiveness
- encourage and enable the development of each member of your team's interpersonal skills
- consider the benefits of introducing incentives which will be seen as rewards for achievement

The *psychological contract* is a continual process of explicit and implicit bargaining, and an individual's perception and expectations have an important influence on their behaviour.

CORE UNIT D1

MANAGE INFORMATION FOR ACTION

D1.1   Gather required information

The quality of a management decision is largely dependent on how good the information is which goes into making that decision. Broadly speaking, there are two types of information generated at work - that which is a result of normal everyday activities and that which is additionally researched or generated for a specific purpose. Record-keeping is about what has been done or has happened in the past and which can provide information to be used to inform future events. The records for which you are likely to be responsible are routine tasks in which data or transactions must be processed so that activities can continue, such as sales orders, job cards, time sheets, employee records. The data needs to be accurate if it is to provide *information* so that action can be taken.

Before designing and setting up recording processes and documents, you should consider what the information will be used for and assess its worth. The value of information lies in the action taken as a result of receiving it. It must have some value otherwise it is not worth the cost of collecting and storing it, and the benefits obtainable from it must also exceed the costs of acquiring it. Before you decide about having more information, you need to decide on the marginal benefits you can expect from getting it and the extra costs of obtaining it. The value of information must relate to the frequency of its provision and to where, in the decision-making process, it will be used - operational, tactical, or strategic decisions.

If you feel there might be a need to improve your recording systems, consider some kind of audit - the scale will depend on the type of information, the context and the implications for other colleagues. The areas you might consider would be to look firstly at your present system to see how the information is obtained, stored, accessed, communicated and used; who is involved in each of these processes and what paperwork is involved; what the time-scales are; whether there is any equipment involved; and who controls each of the processes. Secondly, consider how effective the present system is with regard to reliability, accuracy, comprehension, speed, and cost-effectiveness. Thirdly, see if you can identify the causes of problems with the present system - is the system poorly designed? are there bottlenecks, gaps or missing links? is it because of some human error? is there too much information or inadequate control? You should be able to find the answers to these questions relatively easily by some of these methods - *discussions; interviews; meetings; diary keeping; questionnaires; logging telephone, fax and e-mail usage; reviewing written communications.*

If you decide you do need to design new records think about:

- what information is provided?
- what is it used for?
- who will use it?
- how often?
- does the frequency with which it will be used relate to the frequency with which it will be provided?
- what will be achieved by using it?
- what other relevant information is available which could be used instead?

Wherever there will be a need to analyse information prior to passing it on to other people, you should consider the methods you will use before deciding on how to collect the data. All too frequently managers try to make decisions from information that is not presented in a way that is easy to use. The balance between *quantitative* and *qualitative* information is important. Quantitative data is clearly measurable in numerical terms, whilst qualitative information is difficult to measure - for example the intangible aspects of customer loyalty or employee motivation. When qualitative factors will clearly influence a decision, you should either use your *judgement* and try to balance the quantitative and qualitative factors, or use a technique such as *scalar rankings* or *cost-benefit analysis* for converting qualitative values into quantitative values. These are a few of the more common methods which can be used to collect data for special purposes or non-routine situations:

- *observation*
- *questionnaire (postal or telephone)*
- *interview* (face-to-face or telephone)
- *sampling*
- *random sample*
- *systematic sample*
- *multi-stage sample*
- *stratified sample*
- *quota sample*

- *cluster sample*

Once you have your raw data it is the *interpretation* that is the important aspect of attributing meaning and it is often more meaningful when there has been some discussion with appropriate work colleagues. This is where the qualitative emphasis becomes important. Management skill is about eliciting meanings to help decision-making. The deciding factor in a decision can very often be the interpretation rather than the facts. A persuasive interpretation can sometimes be more successful and is a source of power which managers can use to good effect in many organisational situations

D1.2 Inform and advise others

Good communication is vital to effective team work and if you and your colleagues are to achieve your objectives. You will find yourself communicating with several different types of people - more senior managers, your own work-team, other peer group colleagues, and clients or customers. As a junior manager your role will entail ensuring instructions are carried out willingly and precisely; being loyal and supportive; anticipating your own manager's requirements; being resourceful and showing initiative. If you encourage your work-team to participate in the decision-making process, you should find communications more readily understood and instructions adopted.

The sophistication of communications you use will depend on the nature of what you are trying to get across. It would be inappropriate to spend an hour on preparation every time you make a telephone call. However, a few quick thoughts in advance will prepare you. Sometimes you will know who the recipient of your communication is, sometimes you won't. It could be a customer - known or unknown; it could be a junior member of staff; it could be a senior manager. But, even so, it is important to build up whatever picture you can about them as this will give a *perspective* on the most successful approach to take. Relationships with customers will naturally be more formal.

When either informing or advising other people of something, you must select the method which best suits the situation, the people to receive it, and the type of information. Personal contact in the form of operational meetings, team briefings and informal, but official, face-to-face communication are acknowledged to have advantages over other methods. You can use *language* appropriate to the person you are speaking with, you can use *tone*, *words* or *body language* to emphasise your meaning, you don't have to worry about spelling and punctuation, and other aspects of laying out written work, and you can *see* your impact and get instant *feedback*. The telephone runs a close second. Other oral and/or visual means such as *video/video conferencing, interviews, seminars*, are all effective ways to give and receive information when used appropriately.

If you are invited to make a verbal presentation, plan your ideas carefully. These three stages should help you:

- *Prepare*:
  Have you got all the facts and can you support them?
  What objections might be raised to your ideas?

Can you refute them?

Have you presented all your supporting material, such as costs, duty rosters etc, in an easily understandable way?

Are you sure you have considered all aspects of your plan?

Have you highlighted *sufficiently* the benefits to your organisation by adopting your ideas?

Have you prepared how and what you will say, and made notes to help you?

- *Present your case by*:

Getting to the point quickly

Explaining why you are taking this course of action or making these proposals

Showing any alternatives you have considered and why you have ruled them out

Pointing out the advantages and disadvantages and highlighting the benefits of the advantages

Finally, summarise your argument and don't forget to show the cost, and stress the benefits

- *Handling questions*:

Be prepared to answer questions as these show your listeners are interested in what you have said

Deal with all questions politely and don't feel goaded by criticisms - these can also be positive to your case

Where objections are made, try to show how your proposals can overcome them

There are circumstances when written material is better, such as when communicating *instructions* which have to be followed or which contain *specifications* or complex data; where you may not see the recipient; when something will require referring to frequently; when something applies to several members of your work-team; or when it is vital that there is no misunderstanding. There are many ways of providing written material - *letters, memoranda, reports, summaries, notices, procedures manuals, safety manuals, briefing papers, sales literature, fax, e-mail, Internet and Intranet, viewdata, forms, slide presentations, press releases, adverts* etc. Product and service literature is often prepared with the help of external expertise. Well-designed material is essential if you have a page on the Internet. If your work is office-based, you are increasingly likely to use e-mail. When you are putting forward work *plans*, whether they are for routine activities or for particular projects, check to see:

- they are clear and show a purpose

- they are understandable by all those to be involved in their implementation
- they can easily be amended if circumstances change
- they show how monitoring will take place

Whenever you need to communicate with others be *courteous*; '*listen*' to what the other person's response is - either verbal or written; use a *style* appropriate to the situation and the other person; and think and *plan* your communication -

- Use appropriate *language* and don't use technical jargon as a cover-up for lack of knowledge or to 'fool' the other person
- In a face-to-face situation, don't let mannerisms distract your listener
- Choose an appropriate *time* to get your message across - bad timing can frequently sink otherwise good arguments
- *Structure* your points logically
- *Build* in aspects you know the other person will find positive
- *Define* the other person's role in relation to you

Finally, continue to look for ways to improve communications, since information is abundant from all directions and there is a growing feeling that little of it hits the target.

D1.3 Hold meetings

In today's business world there are many types of meetings, but it's likely that, as a front-line manager, you will mostly be involved with holding routine meetings with your work-team, customers or clients. Meetings are about two or more people meeting face-to-face (in person or video link) to discuss specific topics. Well-run meetings should be an effective way of group communication, generating ideas, negotiating, and team building. If run badly, they can be a waste of time and cause disagreement. Much depends upon the qualities of those taking part and their respective skills in communicating effectively. Sometimes meetings are held which are not always necessary, so you should consider whether an alternative method might be more appropriate for getting information across. Regular meetings can be the worst culprits for wasting time and it takes courage to cancel a meeting.

Any meeting, formal or informal, will be far more effective if those invited know in advance what the purpose is and an indication, in the form of an *agenda*, of what is going to be discussed. The period of notice will depend upon the nature of the meeting, but even relatively impromptu gatherings will be more effective if participants are given, say, half an hour's notice of what the content is to be. You should allow time for preparation by issuing any documents well ahead, with the meeting notification or agenda. Giving out major detailed reports and other documents in the meeting itself makes meaningful discussion im-possible.

The venue is important. A poor room with distractions can lead to a poor meeting. Choose something of an appropriate size that is warm but well-ventilated. Where you are using a meeting room, choose a seating arrangement which reflects the type and status of the meeting - *boardroom, round table, negotiating, freestyle, theatre style, schoolroom, horseshoe, herringbone*. If an office is to be used, make arrangements in advance for telephone calls to be re-directed and dealt with when the meeting is finished.

The way you conduct yourself when you are holding meetings should set an example to the other participants. However informal the meeting or discussion, a few rules will benefit all - obedience to the 'Chair', sticking to the subject, and debating 'through the Chair'. Get to know quickly about the strong points of those present and use their knowledge and skills. Use the skills and knowledge of all participants, listen carefully to what is being said and be fair to all those present in giving a hearing to all points of view, even those with whom you might disagree. Encourage creativity by inviting participants to put ideas forward. If you call for all ideas before inviting criticism of them, there is a greater chance everyone's ideas will be heard. Flip charts are a good way of recording them as they are made. You will find some can quite clearly be ruled out, whilst others will be worth further consideration. This approach is often more successful in preventing lengthy and acrimonious debate which holds back good ideas and, because time will have elapsed since a suggestion was made, debate is likely to be more objective about the issues and not be seen as a personal attack on the participant putting forward a rejected idea. Finally, use time sensibly and learn how to gauge when to stay with an item longer than planned originally or when to move on with items that don't need the planned amount of time.

Taking notes during a meeting needs practice and can be distracting from the discussion. If you are not going to keep notes, arrange for someone else to do it for you - either someone else within the group who has agreed beforehand to do it or a secretary. Arrange for each participant to receive a summary copy afterwards so that you all know what actions have been agreed and need to be followed up and by whom. Keep a file copy for future reference. A successful meeting means its purpose has been met, everyone has had an opportunity to put their contributions forward, and the outcome is broadly acceptable to the majority of participants. Do your meetings achieve this?

OPTIONAL UNIT C7

CONTRIBUTE TO THE SELECTION OF PERSONNEL FOR ACTIVITIES

C7.1 Contribute to identifying personnel requirements

Many organisations draw up annual objectives at their annual budget-setting period, and this will doubtless include a review of staffing requirements during the forthcoming budgetary period. An implicit part of managing is ensuring you have sufficient resources to carry out the activities for which you are responsible. This includes making sure you have sufficient staff with the right knowledge and skills, not only for immediate jobs but also for work that will need to be done during the next, say, three to six months. Unit A1 gives you a few prompts on drawing up your master job/work schedule from which you will be able to see where you are anticipating increases or decreases in work, or whether there are any changes planned. A good starting point is to ask these questions:

- what skills are required?
- what numbers of staff are required with different skills?
- what training is needed?

Your requirements will be the same if no changes are being introduced. However, business rarely stands still and change is part of being responsive to customer requirements. You may need more or less staff, or you may need staff with different skills. This Unit concentrates on changes to the level and types of staffing requirement whilst Unit C9 concentrates on training and development.

At one time most organisations employed either full-time or part-time staff. Now your company may have policies for offering other types of employment contracts; such as temporary, to undertake a specific project contract, or voluntary, for people who want to gain experience within your 'industry'. If your staffing needs could be more appropriately met by non-traditional work arrangements, you should prepare proposals to put forward to discuss with your manager or personnel department.

A 'job' consists of a series of tasks, responsibilities and obligations, for which skills, knowledge, training and development are needed. Different jobs will also require a variety of levels of qualities such as initiative, reliability and ability to withstand stress, physical stamina and mental agility, and the capacity for planning, co-ordinating and managing the work of others. If you work within a large organisation and have a central personnel department, you may be involved in job evaluation from time-to-time. But, this technique does not have to be the preserve of a specialist personnel function, and you could find it valuable in analysing exactly what each job role involves, or should involve.

You should certainly involve your work-team in putting this information together as they will be able to tell you what is likely to work best and what pitfalls should be avoided. Involving them at this planning stage will help them to feel ownership of decisions which are ultimately made. Depending on the type of activities in which you are involved *work study* and *work measurement* might also be useful. If you do use these methods, however, you should make sure you discuss them first with your own manager, since staff might see them as threatening and you could inadvertently cause a dispute. Where you have trade union representation within your company, they will almost certainly wish to be involved in this type of issue.

When putting your proposals forward you should also remember to include costing information as you might need to budget for extra things such as safety training or equipment, or other things which a new employee will need to enable them to be effective in their job. *Negotiating* and presenting your proposals effectively will require you to use *communication* skills effectively. Well-prepared plans and proposals which demonstrate how they support your department or section's work objectives are more likely to get agreement than those which are poorly presented. Negotiating might mean a one-to-one situation with your manager, or it could involve meetings with other colleagues and managers. Make the development of your influencing and persuasion skills part of your commitment to improving your personal competence.

C7.2   Contribute to selecting required personnel

Your company will probably have established selection procedures, with managers being given different levels of responsibility for selecting different categories of employees. Selecting personnel effectively, however, is only possible when the previous planning stages are completed. If your manager encouraged you to participate, you should have been involved in drawing up a *job description* and an *employee specification* so you should be familiar with what you are looking for when applicants provide information about themselves. The job description should specify the job title and provide information about the purpose of the job (ie the reason it exists), the key tasks involved, and the conditions of work such as hours, rate of pay, any special circumstances. An employee specification will provide you with what is needed to do the job effectively.

There is an inherent amount of *stress* in any job, but designing jobs and matching individuals to them can reduce unnecessary stress. A mis-match between an individual and the job itself is an important factor which exacerbates work-related stress. Your responsibility for ensuring a good match between an individual and the job starts at the point of entry to the job. Choosing the right person is easier if you know exactly what the job entails and have identified areas and levels of stress. You may have sometimes to face difficult decisions like continuing temporarily with a vacancy rather than getting the first available individual.

There is no ideal selection process. The best way is to work step-by-step from the employee specification. Focus on the real essentials and make sure that nothing likely to make the difference between success and failure in the job is left unassessed. What kind of evidence will convince you that a candidate does or does not match up? Your selection should not discriminate directly or indirectly in any way, whether it is on the grounds of race or sex, or anything else. Your process should provide opportunities to assess every item within the specification and you should make a systematic evaluation against clear and appropriate criteria and not just on instinct or gut feeling. It should also convey to candidates what it would be like to work for you. Some things will be relatively easy to assess and others will be more difficult. Although a completed application form will be able to provide you with basic information, there are other methods which might be more suitable to find out specific types of information, such as letters of application; curriculum vitae; pre-screening by telephone or questionnaire; first interview to draw up a shortlist; pencil and paper tests; practical tests of manual dexterity or coordination; work samples; trainability tests; personality questionnaires; simulations; second interview; references; medical questionnaire or examination; or an assessment centre combining several of these.

An assessment plan should list a range of competences which are compiled from the employee specification; they are sometimes broken down into essential and desirable. These can then be used to rank or grade each candidate. As well as ensuring candidates have the knowledge and skills necessary to do the 'technical' aspects of the job, many employers now look for key core skills such as an ability to work with others; holding an appropriate level of reading and writing ability; problem-solving skills; number and mathematical ability; listening and speaking skills; ability to work safely; ability to deal with things that happen unexpectedly; and ability to use computers.

Most people have been involved in an *interview* at some stage of their working life. A face-to-face interview gives an opportunity for both the interviewer and the interviewee to ask questions. All interviews follow the same basic principles and structure. The interview should be designed and conducted with methods appropriate to the situation - either formal or informal.

- *Preparation: background data*
  It is advisable to enter the interview with as many of the pertinent facts as possible. In all interview situations it will be necessary to collect information about both the job and its environment, and about the individual to be interviewed. It is also essential that the interviewer has a grasp of the alternative courses of action open to him or her and to the interviewee in terms of company policies and procedures.

- *Preparation: definition of objectives*
  It is essential to determine just what it is hoped that the interview will achieve, and to reaffirm that it is the appropriate tool for the task.

- *Preparation: planning the interview*
  Planning is a two-fold operation: planning of times, location and personnel (followed by administrative arrangements); planning of the shape and form of the interview itself.

- *Preparation: administrative arrangements*
  It is essential to ensure that everything goes according to plan. If interviewers and interviewees are not notified in good time, or are not told where the interview is to take place, things will not go according to plan. Nor will a panel interview go smoothly if the

members of the panel are not properly co-ordinated. A meeting is, therefore, necessary to ensure that all interviewer participants are aware of the interview strategy and know what their specific part in it is to be.

If your own manager is conducting the interviews you may find the administrative arrangements will be delegated to you. This checklist is useful:

- Will the interview location be available at the required time?
- Has the interviewee been notified of the time and place of the interview, the identity of the interviewer(s) and the likely duration of the interview?
- Have any other interviewers been advised of the time and place of the interview and met to discuss their strategy and tactics?
- Has the receptionist been told whom to expect, when and where to direct them?
- Have arrangements been made to prevent interruptions to the interview by telephone calls or personal visits?
- Has everyone had sufficient notice of the event?
- Have appropriate refreshments been arranged, bearing in mind the required formality/informality, interviewee expectations?
- If the interviewee has to travel to the interview, have arrangements been made to recompense him/her?
- If an internal candidate has to absent him or herself from normal duties, has the appropriate manager been contacted?
- Is action in hand to deal with the outcome of the interview - eg has the person responsible for preparing a contract been advised of an impending appointment?

After the interview has been planned and arranged, there still remain some final checks to be made in the interview room immediately before the interview:

- *Avoid*: extremes of heat and cold; chairs which are awkward to get in and out of and inelegant to sit in; confusion over who sits where. Indicate the interviewee's seat clearly to him or her and make sure there are no 'booby traps', eg the wobbly chair
- *Ensure*: adequate ventilation; appropriate seating arrangements; space for the interviewee to put down any papers he or she may have brought; table for coffee cup, etc

There are several alternative strategies that the interviewer can adopt according to their own temperament and the demands of the situation.

Each has its uses in particular circumstances, although some are of more general applicability than others.

- *the frank and friendly strategy* - the essence of which is the 'come on now, tell me all about it' kind of statement; the encouraging nods and remarks and other overt signs of approval
- *the conspiratorial strategy* - 'you can tell me, it will go no further', and 'we'll show them what we can do'; may be useful in encouraging the reticent interviewee
- *the joint problem-solving strategy* - characterised by statements such as, 'well, let's work out how we can cope with that' and an approach which has something in common with both those above
- *the stress strategy* - the interviewee is placed under heavy and remorseless pressure, with opinions challenged, beliefs ridiculed, and his or her achievements belittled. It can very easily backfire.
- *the sweet and sour strategy* - based on the belief the interviewee will give away most about themselves or their problems when they are relaxed. This presupposes the interviewee is more likely to feel relaxed in the interview if the relaxation takes the form of a respite from pressure
- *the tell and sell strategy* - an exposition by the interviewer who attempts, through powers of persuasion, to convince the interviewee that they both want to attain the same objectives
- *the tell and listen strategy* - may be an appropriate half-way house between tell and sell, or alternative courses of action which may be difficult for the interviewee

Finally, you must ensure that you work within both your company's policies and legislative requirements with regard to employment law. You should be especially vigilant with regard to the possibility of discrimination. Being unfamiliar with the law is no protection from prosecution if a candidate feels there is a case to be brought. Make sure your own behaviour and arrangements you make comply with what is required. If you are unsure about anything, discuss it either with your own manager or a personnel specialist.

Your records should record details of the candidates, the processes that were followed, decisions made and the reasons for making them. Your filing system should be able to provide quick and reliable information if there is a need to check back on anything that happened during the recruitment period.

OPTIONAL UNIT C9

CONTRIBUTE TO THE DEVELOPMENT OF TEAMS AND INDIVIDUALS

C9.1 Contribute to the identification of development needs

Setting team and individual development objectives is usually part of a *performance review* system. *Performance appraisal* can provide meaningful opportunities where your staff know they can contribute to both their own and company development. Your organisation's *culture* will determine how effective a process this is. *Appraisal* should be carried out on a regular basis - annually or six-monthly; but progress should be reviewed regularly. It is often viewed with hostility by staff as it is essentially part of a management control system. An organisational culture which has a participatory style and approach to work, and which uses praise and constructive criticism in a supportive way, will encourage openness and determination to develop and help your staff to overcome feelings of being threatened. A culture which militates towards a dictatorial management style is likely to experience difficulty with this approach. Employees are likely to feel threatened and challenged, and unwilling to participate in a committed way. Help your work-team to look upon it as a positive opportunity to review, change, and evaluate, and something which benefits both themselves and the organisation. Your own behaviour needs to be supportive and non-threatening. Your communication skills and understanding of human behaviour are vital to successful review, and appraisal needs to be seen to benefit all members of the workforce alike, be they part of a work group or a management group. If you carry out an assessment interview, emphasise that aims are about mutual planning and problem solving. Make sure you base it on performance and not an individual's personality.

Successful team working is usually the key to achieving business goals, the means of moving your company forward (Units C12 and C15 concentrate more on how teams work). Objectives will help you and your staff to focus on specific activities to achieve them. Effective team-working doesn't just happen though, and you will need to find ways to develop the team itself, as well as the individuals in it. Involve all your team members in evaluating the team's development needs and assess its strengths and weaknesses. If you use an audit approach around, for example, Occupational Standards, you can ask questions such as: do we do it? how do we do it?; do we do it well? do we review it? The activities in your department or section work plan will help you to identify areas where your staff might need some development. It could be because there is some new and unfamiliar equipment or new work methods, or someone is performing badly in their job, or there is a company initiative to raise quality generally. Whatever the reason, the next stage is to develop this by discussing each team member's contribution with them and, between you, identifying where any training or development is needed and how best it can be gained. Encourage them to feel comfortable to ask questions and express their views. Be clear about the objectives of the development plan and balance your business needs with individual aspirations. Once areas for development have been identified you can then agree priorities. You may find this framework useful to help you analyse what your team needs:

- what knowledge, skills and competences are needed by your staff to carry out their jobs effectively?
- what attitudes are necessary for satisfactory performance in various posts?
- what development or training inputs are needed to remedy current deficiencies?

Many organisations are now involved in *Investors in People* (IIP), a government-driven initiative to improve the quality of training and development by linking them with business performance and strategy. Even if your company is not involved in this, it might have its own review processes, whether they are formal in a large company or more informally carried out in a company with just a handful of employees.

If your company has committed itself to developing its employees to National Standards of competence and has a policy for providing employees with an opportunity to take part in an NVQ or SVQ programme, this will make your role somewhat easier than if this is not so. Occupational Standards have been developed for almost all the occupations you could think of and they are benchmarks of good performance achievable by a competent practitioner of that occupation. As a manager, you should audit yourself against the MCI Management Standards to highlight areas which you can use for development. The same audit approach can be used with members of your work-team by using these or any other appropriate Standards; this will give you a structure around which to build individual and team development activities. Much of this process will obviously involve you in communicating with your work-team orally. But you will need to keep written records of what takes place and what agreements and arrangements are made.

A company which offers development opportunities to its staff is a company where people want to work. Personal development should be a continuous commitment as it will help to increase job *motivation* and a commitment to stay. It will enable you to make the best use of available resources and enable your staff to keep pace with the new skill requirements imposed by every-changing products and services.

C9.2   Contribute to planning the development of teams and individuals

Personal development is one way of helping your company attain or keep its competitive edge. The consequences of electing to 'smarten up' your employees rather than 'dumbing them down' will help work output to stand out amongst your competitors. Getting the most from your staff means providing opportunities for them to achieve the development they need. Therefore, training and development should never be regarded as punishment for inadequate performance or staff will resent being put on a programme or refuse to benefit from instruction. The need for development of new skills and the continuous improvement of existing competence should be accepted as a natural feature of working life.

Knowing what skills are going to be needed within your team to cover future work means planning beforehand to make sure that current members of your team develop the skills that will be needed. Many organisations are now *'customer driven'* - whether in manufacturing or provision of services - and this can pose problems of peaks and troughs in demand which you will need to manage effectively. This could mean that your company has a core of permanent staff and a policy for recruiting others when required, such as contracts for specific projects, temporary contracts for specified duration and hours, and opportunities for voluntary work. 'Buying-in' staff to cover a specific contingency is referred to in Unit C7. If you work with this type of situation you are likely to be faced with challenges to integrate new employees into the team. You might look at providing a regular *'induction'* package to help provide consistent introduction to your company for all new staff. This would cover things such as health and safety procedures, work methods, or other company policies. Talk this type of thing through with your manager and put forward new ideas if you think you could make improvements to existing arrangements. New technology carries with it the demand for new skills and knowledge, but it does not determine which individuals should have acquired which skills and knowledge. That determination depends upon your company's policy for making the best use of its people. A company which competes on the basis of quality of service needs to be assiduous in ensuring that new skills and knowledge permeate the company. Quality has to be built in to every step of the process.

MCI's checklist approach is helpful when drawing up an action plan for your team's work activities which you can then use to help identify training or development needs for both team and individuals:

- List out the key activities which you and your team are going to be involved in, say, over the next three to six months
- Using an overview of the NVQ/SVQ level 3 Management Standards, match these activities against the elements which appear to be relevant
- Use the performance criteria in the elements to help you carry out these activities
- Draw up an action plan to help you manage the work

Although your plans will be to meet your own section or department's work commitments, it must be within an integrated framework of your company's overall human resource development. When you are putting plans forward, it is likely you will be asked to consider issues such as *multi-skilling* or bringing in people from other sections or departments. These are both ways of ensuring staff and skills are used in the most cost-effective way. Proposals for development activities will need to show how they contribute to meeting work objectives, the levels of expertise required together with the expected standards of performance, the ways it will best be achieved (eg *training courses*, *coaching*, *group activities*, etc), and the time it will take and the costs involved. You should also attempt to show what the costs and other consequences would be if staff were not competent, or you needed to recruit externally to get the skills needed. Two other important aspects to which you must pay attention are *equal opportunities* and *discrimination*. Your practices must not discriminate in any way with regard to development opportunities. In fact, these aspects of the law are often overlooked in everyday work practices and they are something you may need to consider including within all personal development plans. When you have finalised your plans you will most likely be asked to provide details in the form of a report which will be considered by more senior managers or personnel specialists if your organisation is large and has a personnel department. Alternatively, you might be asked to attend a meeting or prepare a brief presentation to support your proposals.

The drawing up and agreeing *personal development plans* or *learning contracts* as part of an appraisal process is a recognised method of formalising the commitment by staff and their managers to the development process. Make sure your staff understand their development goals and agree start and end dates, with agreed reviews in between.

C9.3   Contribute to development activities

Understanding how different people learn is essential if you are to help your work-team members to develop their own potential. Many people learn and develop by experience and everyone has their own preferred learning style and different starting point. Learning from experience is a continuous cycle - it could be from new methods of doing something at work, a demonstration or presentation, or simply a discussion, after which comes a period of reflection on what has happened. People also learn from social activities outside work and bring this new knowledge and experience into the workplace. This type of learning can be just as effective when someone is able to provide the bridge and help them to transfer their learning into a work environment. NVQ/SVQ candidate packs often give guidance on using a personal development plan and this is useful in helping to build up a *portfolio* of evidence and achievement.

Training courses are only one way of meeting development needs. Sometimes you might need to give some *instruction*, or offer *coaching* or give a *presentation* to your group. Your choice needs to be appropriate to the situation and the individuals involved. You are likely to be most involved in *on-the-job training* rather than away from the workplace. Training courses and lectures away from work have a useful part to play in development, but people can sometimes have difficulty in applying what they have learnt to their own work environment and job situation. *Mentoring* and *coaching* are increasingly being used to provide support and to help people improve their performance. Focused coaching is systematic and methodical, and requires both the coach and learner to concentrate on the task in hand and be willing to devote time to developing the skills. If you undertake coaching with members of your work-team, you might find it useful to use the Units on coaching or facilitation of learning through demonstration and instruction within the National Standards for Training and Development. Some Modern Apprenticeships include these Units within their frameworks. *Job rotation* programmes are useful in enabling employees to acquire an overall understanding of the organisation. Group training which encourages people to learn from each other through discussing issues, pooling experiences and critically examining opposing viewpoints include *case studies, business games, T-groups,* and *role play* exercises which are useful when you are trying to build up a team spirit. Off-the-job methods which have a role to play in providing underpinning and supporting knowledge could be *programmed learning* or *open learning* packages, or *interactive video*. *Virtual reality* is playing an increasingly important role in preparing staff for potentially life-threatening situations.

When you are involved in delivering any type of development activity, you need to be able to put learners at their ease, to sequence and pace information, and to use language appropriate to each learner and situation. If it is appropriate to *demonstrate* how or why something is done, choose a method which is as realistic as possible (with due regard to cost). Make sure both you and those who will imitate you follow good practice and adhere to health and safety legislation. Use questions to see how much understanding has been acquired and make sure no one is able to put either themselves or others at risk. Match coaching opportunities with individual learning needs and learning objectives. Give constructive *feedback* and provide opportunities for practice. If you feel someone's learning is being inhibited, look for ways together which might help them to overcome it.

As work pressures increase, people are likely to feel some stress. One real way to reduce stress for your staff is to learn to manage your own time effectively and to help them learn the same skill. Time management is about making the best use of time and decreasing the distractions and time-wasting activities. There are various time management techniques which you could look at to help both you and your staff but, basically, they fall into the categories of knowing how individuals function best, the matching of skills held and skills needed, and effective scheduling. Next time you are involved in planning work schedules, or staff reviews, you might be able to find ways of reducing stress levels created by poorly managed time.

Finally, help your staff to be able to practice and apply their learning to maintain their momentum and motivation. It is not always possible to make monetary rewards, but job enrichment and personal achievement are likely to help today's employees maintain their 'employability' in the future.

C9.4 Contribute to the assessment of people against development objectives

National Occupational Standards, NVQs, SVQs, and the Modern Apprenticeship are good starting points for identifying, defining and assessing the competences and learning abilities of individuals. The Department for Education and Employment defines competence as 'The ability to perform the activities within an occupational area to the levels of performance expected in employment'. National Occupational Standards and the NVQ/SVQs specify in detail what a proficient member of staff ought to be able to achieve in their particular job. National Occupational Standards are a vital source of information because they set out what a member of your staff should know and should be able to do in practical terms in the workplace. They state clearly the tasks to be done, under what circumstances, and to what standard. And they include precise criteria by which you can judge whether or not this is happening. Organisations can freely 'mix and match' any Units from any occupational areas to meet their own tailored requirements for individual jobs. Standards can be used in any organisation whatsoever, independently of the NVQ/SVQ system and its formal assessment requirements.

If you work closely with your work-team you should have an established rapport and be well-placed to make assessments about each individual's performance. *Appraisal interviews* are a common two-way process in which a manager and appraisee reach agreement on areas for development. Even if your company has informal arrangements, a structured approach will help managers to look at how far each individual has achieved his or her work objectives and help them to find out about their personal development achievements. Your company might have an agreed appraisal method that fits with its culture, structure and size, and you will work within that structure. Each system has its merits and combining two or more methods may provide an optimum system for your company.

Assessment is invariably already an integral part of human resource development systems in practice, whether it is formally called assessment or not. Frequently, existing systems can be used and enhanced by adopting the Occupational Standards or NVQs and SVQs to give clear structure and specification to staff appraisal and development. If employees are registered as NVQ or SVQ candidates, you can give them an opportunity to become involved in gaining qualifications which are formally assessed to a national Standard. The new Modern Apprenticeship scheme formalises apprentice training in the context of NVQs or SVQs and each apprentice who successfully completes will receive an NVQ/SVQ at level 3. As a lot of the assessment will need to be carried out on your premises, appropriately skilled and experienced staff will need to be trained as formal assessors. Formal assessors are required to be qualified in the relevant NVQ/SVQ units for *assessors* and *advisers* (Training & Development D32, D33). If you are involved in contributing to the assessment process you might play a part in *coaching* members of your work-team. Or, in a more informal way, you can also play an important part by being a *mentor* to another employee.

There are other methods of assessing employees against development objectives and some companies favour *free reports* where each individual manager decides what to put in and what to stress. Others find a *grade/rank system* more suitable to their needs whereby a manager ranks each employee in order of merit. A *rating system* which brings out an individual's strengths and weaknesses is sometimes suitable to identify training requirements. *Behaviour expectation scales* is a development of the checklist approach, assessing aspects of performance in particular job dimensions. *Self-assessment* and *peer group assessment* are two other methods which are increasingly used as they provide opportunities for a more diverse assessment.

Evidence of competence is about outcomes of an activity. Involvement in assessing people means collecting information from an appropriate variety of sources. You might get it from looking at a finished product or outcome of someone's work to assess whether it meets the specification and standard set; or you could get it from actually observing how an individual carries out a task; you can get it from asking other people who have been part of the process and had some involvement with the person you are assessing. You need to record this information and use it as a basis for review. When you pass on this information to someone else who may have a more formal assessment role, you must make sure that you do not introduce any personal bias into it, either for or against an individual, or put your own views forward rather than those you are assessing. When you are making an assessment you must ensure the work is actually that of the person being assessed and that it meets all the criteria which have previously been decided on as essential to a competent worker in the job. If it doesn't, that will be the area for discussing with an individual or work-team how they can go about making further progress towards the goals they have set. Set aside specific pockets of time where each of you can devote time to reflecting on achievements, identifying where things haven't quite gone according to plan, what new learning needs there are and what aspirations need to be met. Remember, it is a two-way process and if your staff members are to gain from it, they need to feel at ease in being able to recognise where improvement might be required, or further work to be done. Each individual should be in a position to make informed decisions about their own assessment and learning needs. They need to be able to work with you to identify the best opportunities to collect evidence to show that they have the appropriate knowledge and understanding to underpin their performance. *Feedback* on achievements must be constructive; otherwise staff are likely to be switched off by the process.

Managers involved in any of these methods need to be appropriately trained themselves beforehand. The approach to appraisal interviews is very much akin to *counselling* and the style you adopt will depend on your personal preference, the nature of your relationship with each individual employee, and your skill level in a counselling type of situation. With all these systems, you must apply identical criteria to the assessment of each individual in a particular job grade, use all available information, and be as objective as you can in interpreting that information. It can be all too easy to reach conclusions about someone before you have heard their input, so you should always make sure there are opportunities for staff to question and challenge the accuracy or relevance of the assessment itself or the criteria on which it is based. If you want to look further at how you could meet the National Standards for planning, delivering or assessing training and development you should contact your regional NCVQ (QCA) office, SQA, or your local TEC.

OPTIONAL UNIT C12

LEAD THE WORK OF TEAMS AND INDIVIDUALS TO ACHIEVE THEIR OBJECTIVES

C12.1 Plan the work of teams and individuals

To get the best from your staff you need to have regard both for the individuals within your work-teams and for the tasks which they need to accomplish. Do you know what a successful or an unsuccessful team actually looks like? Effective team-working needs an environment in which all members feel comfortable working together and each person is making an equal and relevant contribution. Your management style is critical to successful relationships with your staff. A number of factors have combined to create resistance against autocratic styles of leadership, including changes in society's value system and broader standards of education. Therefore, your style needs to reflect the 1990s. There are a number of things you can do as a manager to help your staff - be loyal; find an acceptable balance between being *employee-centred* and *task-centred*; show concern for safety, health and welfare; meet individual's needs; manage team development.

Day-to-day management will involve you in directing work, developing individuals, criticising, introducing and managing change. Directing work will involve you in helping people to plan deadlines and objectives. Try to make sure they are reasonable and achievable. Setting objectives which are reasonable, but stretching, is one way to provide the challenge which many people find necessary. A practical way in which you can reduce pressure on people is to help them to control their time effectively. Confusing the urgent with the important are real problems for many people. You can help by agreeing priorities with your staff. You will find more about planning in Unit A1 and C4 and C9 will also provide you with information about work-teams.

Although there is no such thing as perfection in communication, it is something everyone has to work at. An appropriate communication *network* will help to bond work-teams together under your leadership. Where you have part-time, temporary or other sub-contracted staff working for you, you will probably need to consider additional mechanisms for helping integration with your more permanent staff.

Their levels of interaction are determined by how communication channels are structured. Maintaining the trust of all your workforce and enabling them to contribute to a successful business, means looking for ways to improve personal relationships. Examine the interaction of your own workforce in the light of these types of networks:

- *the wheel (or star)* - where there is a central link person who has the highest level of satisfaction
- *the circle* - useful in solving complex problems, but tends to experience erratic performance
- *the network* - gives opportunities for full discussion and participation, and works best where a high level of interaction is required
- *Y or chain* - useful for simple problem-solving tasks requiring little interaction among group members

It is important formally to build in time during work schedules to exchange views and ideas. Whilst it may be appropriate to hold a formal meeting with a pre-determined agenda, it is also acceptable, in appropriate situations, to use rather more informal ways of exchanging ideas and views. The more supportive your company's cultural system, the easier you will find it to encourage staff participation. With a more directive and dictatorial approach you are likely to have more difficulty in generating trust and responsibility for work. Consequently, your management approach must take account not only of the need to have *systems*, but also of the *human* and *social factors* as well. With recession and the development of more demanding approaches to management of the workforce, increasing numbers of employees have all too frequently been the butt of unfair practices. Aggressive and unreasonable behaviour at work is not just plain bad management, it is also bad for business. Two pieces of legislation which impinge on equal opportunities, harassment and bullying are the Race Relations Act and the Sex Discrimination Act, plus Codes of Practice covering equal treatment. If someone suffers a detriment or intimidation as a result of their race or sex, they can make a claim under these Acts. Examine your own management behaviour to ensure that you are not unwittingly bullying or harassing members of your staff. Learn to recognise any signs shown by any of your staff or peers.

An organisational culture which has a participatory style and approach to work, and which uses praise and constructive criticism in a supportive way will encourage openness and determination to develop and help your staff to overcome feelings of being threatened. Team-working poses both a serious problem and a great opportunity. Whilst teams involve complex dynamics, they also offer a chance to transform organisational effectiveness in the longer term.

C12.2 Assess the work of teams and individuals

Appraisal and assessment is often viewed with hostility by staff as it is essentially part of a management control system. Your organisation's *culture* will determine how effective a process this is overall. A culture which militates towards a dictatorial management style is likely to experience difficulty. Employees are likely to feel threatened and challenged, and unwilling to participate in a committed way.

The purpose of assessing achievement is to improve future effectiveness. Assessment is invariably already an integral part of human resource development systems in practice, whether is it formally called assessment or not. National Occupational Standards, NVQs, SVQs, and the Modern Apprenticeship are good starting points for identifying, defining and assessing the competences and learning abilities of individuals. The Department for Education and Employment defines competence as 'The ability to perform the activities within an occupational area to the levels of performance expected in employment'. National Occupational Standards are a vital source of information because they set out what a member of your staff should know and should be able to do in practical terms in the workplace. They state clearly the tasks to be done, under what circumstances, and to what standard. And they include precise criteria by which you can judge whether or not this is happening. Organisations can freely 'mix and match' any Units from any occupational areas to meet their own tailored requirements for individual jobs. Standards can be used in any organisation whatsoever, independently of the S/NVQ system and its formal assessment requirements.

Frequently, existing organisational systems can be used and enhanced by adopting the Occupational Standards or NVQs/SVQs to give clear structure and specification to staff appraisal and development. *Appraisal interviews* are a common two-way process in which a manager and appraissee reach agreement on areas for development. The roles associated with helping an NVQ or SVQ candidate through the development process are:

- *adviser* - who helps an individual to identify the most relevant NVQ/SVQ or Units, to seek existing evidence of their competence, to form an action plan for personal development to achieve competence
- *assessor* - who works with an individual to identify specific viable assessment opportunities and plan the collection of a combination

of evidence to meet S/NVQ requirements as efficiently and cost-effectively as possible

- *mentor* - an informal supporter of the candidate and someone who can help in innumerable ways, from being a counsellor, an 'opener of doors', a confidant and friend

Evidence of competence is about outcomes of an activity. Each of your employees will have different levels of confidence and experience in feeling able to take an active part in their own assessment. Always emphasise that aims of assessment are about mutual planning and problem-solving. You need to encourage your staff to take part in ways which do not inhibit or hinder them in putting *evidence* of competence forward to be assessed. This obviously means that, as an assessor, you need to be fully experienced yourself in the occupation you are assessing, to know what the evidence requirements are, and to understand why it is important to make an accurate judgement against only the criteria specified. You need to know how to check the *authenticity* (it really *is* the work of the person being assessed), *validity* (it is relevant to the Standards and meets all the performance criteria), and *sufficiency* (the overall combination of authentic and valid evidence presented is sufficient to establish current competence). If you are assessing someone by observing them, do it as unobtrusively as you can. You might need to include judgements that have been made by other people, such as other members of the work-team or other managers. In these cases you will need to be able to attribute some sort of weighting to its contribution to the overall sufficiency of evidence. Finally, make sure you base assessment on performance and not an individual's personality. If you do need clarification, don't be afraid to talk it through with the employee concerned - communication is a two-way process. If you need to seek outside opinion, remember to work within the parameters of confidentiality that have been established at the outset.

There are other systems of assessing employees against development objectives and some companies favour *free reports*, where each individual manager decides what to put in and what to stress. Others find a *grade/rank system* more suitable to their needs whereby a manager ranks each employee in order of merit. A *rating system* which brings out an individual's strengths and weaknesses is sometimes suitable to identify training requirements. *Behaviour expectation scales* is a development of the checklist approach, which assesses aspects of performance in particular job dimensions. *Self-assessment* and *peer group assessment* are two other methods which are increasingly used as they provide opportunities for a more diverse assessment.

Managers involved in any of these methods, however, need to be appropriately trained beforehand. The approach to appraisal interviews is very much akin to *counselling* and the style you adopt will depend on your personal preference, the nature of your relationship with each individual employee, and your skill level in a counselling type situation. With all these systems, you must apply identical criteria to the assessment of each individual in a particular job grade, use all available information, and be as objective as you can in interpreting that information. It can be all too easy to reach conclusions about someone before you have heard their input, so you should always make sure there are opportunities for staff to question and challenge the accuracy or relevance of the assessment itself or the criteria on which it is based.

Many organisations use teams and it is sometimes difficult to isolate an individual's contribution. Team appraisals need to supplement individual appraisals. Effectiveness does not just happen though, and you will need to find ways to develop the team itself, as well as the individuals in it. Involve all your team members in evaluating the team's development needs and assess its strengths and weaknesses. If you use an audit approach around, for example, Occupational Standards, you can ask questions such as: do we do it? how do we do it?; do we do it well? do we review it? The activities in your department or section work plan will help you to identify areas where your staff might need some development. It could be because there is some new and unfamiliar equipment or new work methods, or someone is performing badly in their job, or there is a company initiative to raise quality generally. Whatever the reason, the next stage is to develop this by discussing each team member's contribution with them and, between you, identify where any training or development is needed and how best it can be gained. Encourage them to feel comfortable to ask questions and express their views. You may find this framework useful to help you analyse what your team needs:

- what knowledge, skills and competences are needed by your staff to carry out their jobs effectively?
- what attitudes are necessary for satisfactory performance in various posts?
- what development or training inputs are needed to remedy current deficiencies?

Be clear about the objectives of the development plan and balance your business needs with individual aspirations. Once areas for development have been identified you can then agree priorities.

C12.3 Provide feedback to teams and individuals on their work

Teams often perceive themselves to be under-performing but when the reasons for this are examined in more depth, it is often that team members report a lack of appreciation. Do you pay enough time to celebrating success or giving adequate recognition to team achievements? If you are to help your work-team to look on assessment as a positive activity within the cycle of review, change, assessment, evaluation, and something which benefits both themselves and the organisation, you need to *reward* their efforts by recognising these sorts of things. Give praise and encouragement when progress has been made. It can be done formally or informally, even within a formally-established system. As long as it is clear, constructive, meets each individual's needs and is appropriate to his or her level of confidence, you can build it into your development cycle.

You need to collect and analyse all the information that has been recorded about your work-team and use it as a basis for feedback and review. If other people have been involved in the assessment process you need to make sure their input is included within the overall 'package' and not either simply ignored or used as a means of creating friction. *Peer group assessment* is a new concept to many employees and some employees may feel threatened by this approach. It must be done within an overall company policy which encourages this type of interaction and has the appropriate mechanisms of support in place.

Your communication skills and understanding of human behaviour are essential ingredients in helping staff to see the benefits whether they are part of a work group or a management group. The way in which you offer criticism is an important factor in minimising stress. Your behaviour needs to be supportive and non-threatening. Staff assessment and appraisal systems are based on the need to keep people informed of how they are doing and this is most effective if they receive *feedback* as things occur. Saving things up for a once-a-year session of retrospective recrimination is a real de-motivator. If you are dissatisfied with someone's performance or behaviour, discuss it at the time. Criticism is hard for anyone to take. It is less stressful and much more useful if it is constructive, backed up by specific examples, linked to agreed standards, and linked to finding a solution. People are often very clear in their own mind about their shortcomings and most people are very willing to try to improve an unsatisfactory situation. Use criticism constructively as a way to improve performance and solve problems.

Make sure you give an appropriate length of time and choose a place which suits each individual, your work requirements and the nature of the feedback. One-to-one feedback is best done out of hearing of fellow workers, although there might be circumstances to give praise discreetly when other people are around. The nature of feedback to groups depends on the situation. A routine team meeting might be appropriate for on-going development. If there has been a specific training activity, it might need a specially-organised feedback session. Don't forget to record the information and ensure that it is only given to people who have authorisation to receive it.

Help your staff to recognise their achievements and sustain their *motivation* to achieve other targets or aspirations. Progressive organisations see managers as supporters of front-line staff, not controllers. Do you have the confidence to ask your staff 'What is it that I'm doing that is hindering your performance?' and to act on the feedback you receive?

OPTIONAL UNIT C15

RESPOND TO POOR PERFORMANCE IN THE TEAM

C15.1 Help team members who have problems affecting their performance

You need to encourage all your staff to pull their weight if you are to have a fully functioning team. Do you have people who don't meet deadlines, cause conflict, make excuses, lack necessary skills, don't respect you, drain your time and energy? If so, you have some classic problems on your hands. Problem employees can bring down morale, destroy productivity and distract you and others from important projects unless they are dealt with quickly and confidently.

Stress from the job itself might be one cause of problems. You can have little practical effect on the factors outside work which are potentially stressful for the people who work for you. You can, however, have an effect upon their place of work. Watch for signs of undue stress and either take steps to help an individual yourself or help by calling in support and practical assistance from more specialised colleagues. In addition to factors concerning the job itself, stress at work can be caused by the environment in which people work. For example, poor lighting, poor ventilation, high noise levels, etc. If you spot what seems to be stress, sometimes you will have to use your knowledge of the individual and the circumstances to help you decide what action to take. In terms of work-related stress, remember that while you may not feel you are making unreasonable demands on your staff, they may find difficulty in being able to tell you. Noting the signs of stress can help you to recognise when all is not well at work.

Counselling has become increasingly important as a means of solving problems jointly. The need is normally prompted by an employee demonstrating they have difficulties in meeting or maintaining the expectations of the job role, either as a result of difficulties within the work environment itself, or personal problems affecting the standard of work. A good manager should consider counselling before the problem becomes acute. Although there may be special cases where a fully-trained counsellor would be more appropriate, as long as you follow the guidelines of help and confidentiality you should be able to carry out a constructive meeting. Where you become involved in counselling someone instead of instigating disciplinary proceedings, make sure the employee is fully aware of the potential seriousness of the situation. Whatever the outcome, counselling should focus on the future - the way forward - and not dwell on the past.

If you find you have to deal with someone who always seems to be doing other things in work time except the things they should be doing or incurring expenses for personal use such as making extensive long-distance phone calls, you will know how difficult it can be to find the right approach to tackle them about it. Try to find out how you can motivate them to work harder. Ask them what their three wishes would be for making their life better at work - if they find work so boring they need to escape at every opportunity, there must be something wrong. Try and find out what it would take to focus their concentration on the job at hand. Perhaps they are simply frustrated because they have been shown no prospects of advancement. It is possible their ideas could boost your business. Try to find out three things they would do if they were in charge. Listen to what they have to say - they may have some valuable ideas about the way your business runs and something you could use. Once they feel ownership of an idea and you put it to use, they may start taking work more seriously. Tackle problems rather than leaving them to get bigger:

- recognise problems early; it's easier to do something before a situation escalates and gets out of hand
- pinpoint the problems of poor performers so you can help them focus on vital improvement areas and prepare yourself to confront a problem employee
- approach poor performers in a way that minimises accusations, hostility and defensiveness - without placing blame
- set realistic, clear performance standards, create an improvement plan together and get your employee to commit to it
- coach the individual to encourage steady progress
- document each step in the process

Keep accurate records for following up the outcome of the situation and use them for follow-up sessions with the employee.

C15.2 Contribute to implementing disciplinary and grievance procedures

You should never ignore or trivialise a grievance put to you. Employees don't raise grievances they don't feel to be important to them. Act promptly and take the matter seriously. When discipline is involved, there will be specified procedures for your organisation and you must follow these procedures. There is no legal requirement for an organisation to have a formal grievance procedure. Many companies have the same procedures for both grievance and discipline but ideally they should be treated in a different manner. It is sensible to follow national Codes of Practice and, if your company has Trade Union involvement, you must ensure you work within these predetermined procedures. With grievance, unlike a disciplinary situation, however, there is no presumption of anybody's 'guilt'.

Grievances often arise from misunderstandings and breakdowns of communications. Minor problems should be easily settled. More serious grievances, though, can arise from anger and frustration within the individual. These cases can often be more complex and require you to involve more senior managers or personnel specialists. When deciding what to do, don't use a large hammer to crack a small nut; keep things in perspective and act accordingly. With a minor grievance based entirely on relationships within the department, you will be the person best placed to deal with it, at least in the first instant. The first time the grievance is brought to you it is likely you will have little prior knowledge of the situation and, thus, be unable to prepare. However, you should be fully conversant with your company's policies and procedures. There are several alternative interview strategies that you can use according to the demands of the situation, your own temperament, and what is acceptable to those who have authorised you to conduct the interview. Probably the most relevant in these types of situations is the *joint problem-solving strategy* (characterised by statements such as, 'well, let's work out how we can cope with that') - an approach which has something in common with both the *frank and friendly strategy* and the *conspiratorial strategy*.

In both grievance and disciplinary situations it is not recommended that you use *the stress strategy* where the interviewee is placed under heavy and remorseless pressure, with opinions challenged, beliefs ridiculed, and his/her achievements belittled; it can very easily backfire. You should find this framework useful in a first grievance situation:

- Ask the complainant to define the situation and what he or she would like done to resolve the problem
- Try to understand why the individual has complained
- Explore the facts
- Attempt to define the real nature of the problem
- If there is still disagreement, isolate the differences - state your position clearly and simply
- Decide if there is a real problem identified
- If yes, suggest a solution
- If no, explain your reasons carefully for rejecting the complaint

The extent to which you can settle grievances depends on how much authority has been delegated to you. Where individual grievances raise issues of fundamental principle within the company, there should be a mechanism for transferring these matters to another forum where different procedures apply, such as *collective bargaining* in situations where there is union recognition within the company.

It is the responsibility of management to ensure that *disciplinary* practices and procedures are effective, fair, well-understood and consistently applied. Your own organisation's senior managers must decide what procedures and practices suit its own circumstances. Large complex organisations will probably need more formal disciplinary procedures whilst a simple straightforward procedure will be adequate for a small company. Whichever situation, they should be applied fairly and consistently with the aim of reducing the need for dismissals. A disciplinary procedure provides a method of dealing with any shortcomings in conduct or performance, and can help a poorly performing employee to become effective again.

Deal with problems early when it is easier to nip them in the bud. Find out all the relevant facts promptly, before memories fade. Talk to the employee, talk to any witnesses, gather statements (if appropriate in serious cases), look at the employee's previous record. Keep an open mind, be consistent with other company practices, stay calm, and follow the *principles of natural justice*.

Make sure you are not only familiar with all the relevant legislation relating to disciplinary situations, but that you know your own organisation's rules and procedures. You should ensure you only work within the level of authority given to you and don't be tempted to overstep the mark. If in doubt, talk with your own manager or personnel department. If the provisions of an agreed disciplinary procedure are ignored when dismissing an employee, this in itself is likely to have a bearing on the outcome of any subsequent complaint of unfair dismissal brought by the employee. The ACAS Code of Practice and Advisory Handbook 'Discipline at Work' provide sound practical advice.

If you are conducting a disciplinary interview with another manager, you should meet beforehand and go through the issues before you and consider what questions to ask and how to ask them. This will have a bearing on the level of contact, content and control that is achieved. A good interview technique is to keep to a *logical sequence*; *link* questions; *avoid* multiple questions; *avoid* ambiguous questions; *steer clear* of jargon; *summarise* regularly. You should:

- ask *open questions*
- ask *probing questions*
- *encourage* the interviewee to talk
- *keep* the conversation flowing
- *avoid* asking yes/no questions
- *avoid* leading questions
- *avoid* interrupting
- *avoid* overt or implied criticism
- *be tactful* in difficult areas
- *avoid* extreme mannerisms
- *look* interested
- *listen*
- *don't* sit and study papers on your desk

It is essential you keep well-documented records of all stages in the disciplinary process - they may be required if the case is taken to an *Industrial Tribunal*. Your records are likely to consist of written notes of meetings or interviews, statements, and other evidence, and it may be appropriate to use tape recordings where their use has been agreed. You will also need to use them as part of your monitoring process for following up the outcome of the situation and improvement of the individual. Focus on the way forward, give support and encouragement, and give praise for improvement.

GLOSSARY

ACAS	Advisory Conciliation and Arbitration Service
CPA	Critical Path Analysis
IIP	Investors In People
IMI	Institute of the Motor Industry
JIT	Just In Time
MBO	Management by Objectives
MCI	Management Charter Initiative
NCVQ	National Council for Vocational Qualifications
NVQ	National Vocational Qualification
PERT	Programme Evaluation and Review Technique
QCA	Qualifications and Curriculum Authority
SCOTVEC	Scottish Vocational Education Council
SPC	Statistical Process Control
SQA	Scottish Qualifications Authority
SVQ	Scottish Vocational Qualification
VDU	Visual Display Unit

INDEX

video/video conferencing/interviews/ seminars 38
recording 57, 67

interviews
  appraisal 56, 58
  grievance/disciplinary 72
  preparation
    administrative arrangements 46-7
    background data 46
    definition of objectives 46
    final room checks 47
    planning the interview 46
  strategies 47-8
    conspiratorial 48
    frank and friendly 48
    joint problem-solving 48
    stress 48
    tell and listen 48
    tell and sell 48

K
knowledge workers 27

L
leadership 26
learning contracts 53

M
management 26
  style 28-9, 49
    communication network 59-60
    dictatorial 60
    employee-centred 59
    participatory 11, 21, 26, 30, 49, 60
    task-centred 59
  systems

communication 5-6
decision-making 2
input 1
output 1
planning 2
problem-solving 2
process 1
quality analysis 4-5
scheduling 3-4
work conditions 4
work-measurement 4
MCI Management Standards 24, 27, 50, 53

meetings
  agenda 41
  participation 42
  pre-scheduled/informal 10
  recording 42
  rules 41-2
  seating 41
  summary copies 42
  time 41-2
  venue 41
method study 4
Modern Apprenticeship scheme 54, 56-7, 62

N
National Occupational Standards 50, 56, 58, 62
network analysis 15
NVQs/SVQs 23-4, 50, 56-8, 62

O
objectives 2, 10, 14, 19, 26
  effectiveness 11
  monitoring 10

76

performance review 10-11
preparation 11-12

P

personal development 23-5
colleagues/teams relationship
28-31
continuous improvement 52
minimisation of team conflict 33-4
monitoring/reviewing 24
objectives 26-7
reflective analysis 24
self-analysis 23-4
storyboard approach 24
trust/support of manager 32
personnel development
activities 54-5
appraisal interviews 56, 58
assessment 56-7, 56-8
behaviour expectation scales 57
free reports 57
grade/rank system 57
information 57-8
peer group 57
self-assessment 57
feedback 58
mentoring 57
motivation 69
planning 52-3
setting team/individual objectives
49-50
training/opportunities 50-2, 56-7
personnel requirements
identification 43-4
selection 45-6
discrimination 48
induction packages 7-8, 52
interviews 46-7
legislation 48

record keeping 48
planning 1, 2, 12-13, 15, 26
action 10, 53
contingency 14
departmental/section/unit 15
forecasting 16
handling questions 12-13, 18, 39
participation 30
preparation 12, 17, 38-9
presentation 12, 17-18, 39-40
team 53
problem-solving
analyse situation 2
consideration of possible solutions
2
counselling approach 64, 68-9
data/information collection 2
psychological contract 34

Q

quality 52
analysis
inspection 4
statistical/graphical method 5
systematic approach 4-5

R

Race Relations Act 30, 60
record keeping 35, 69
accurate 20
grievance/disciplinary procedure
72
individual/team communications
50-1
information flow 20
meetings 42
personnel selection 48
physical work 20
redesigning 36